LITERARY APPRECIATIONS

LITERARY APPRECIATIONS

BY

GEORGE McLEAN HARPER

Essay Index Reprint Series

 BOOKS FOR LIBRARIES PRESS
FREEPORT, NEW YORK

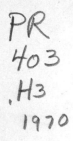

INTERNATIONAL STANDARD BOOK NUMBER:

0-8369-1754-5

LIBRARY OF CONGRESS CATALOG CARD NUMBER:

74-117802

PRINTED IN THE UNITED STATES OF AMERICA

To

JOHN HOWELL WESTCOTT III

To JOHN HOWELL WESTCOTT III was given the honour of serving as a private soldier in the Great War and of laying down his life for the Great Cause. When we are tempted to question whether it was really a cause worth all the sacrifices made to it, when the principles for which so much was offered are obscured and the victory for which we strove appears so much less satisfying than we had anticipated, it will be well to remember in what spirit he and others like him faced the future. Unless we are willing now to believe as firmly and risk as much as they believed and risked, we shall not dare to remember our dead; their idealism will be a reproach to us. It is in any case a challenge.

Taking this young soldier as a representative of many, let us ask why he volunteered and what he hoped the fruits of victory would be.

He was the only son of John Howell Westcott, professor of Latin in Princeton University, and of Edith Flagg Sampson. His father's first American progenitors came to this country from Devonshire in 1638, and his mother was a descendant of John

[v]

and Priscilla Alden, who came over in the *Mayflower*. One of his great-great-grandfathers on the paternal side was William Rush, the sculptor, who was a first cousin of Dr. Benjamin Rush, one of the signers of the Declaration of Independence. Born October 9, 1896, he was prepared for college at Miss Fine's School in Princeton, at the Hoosick School, and at the Hill School. In these boyhood years he was more than once taken abroad, and thus acquired early that sense of the reality of a world other than our own country which most American children gain but slowly, if at all. His horizon was widened, his sympathies were developed, and he possessed, even as a boy, a largeness of political understanding which many men never acquire. For France he entertained a peculiar affection, and in England naturally he felt at home. She was for him indeed the mother country and not foreign or strange. One result of his enjoying the advantages of travel abroad was a knowledge of architecture quite unusual in one so young, and it seems probable that, had he lived, he would have become an architect.

In the summer of 1914, having passed the examinations for entrance to Princeton University, he was studying in Brussels when the German armies invaded Belgium; and returning home through

England he brought with him a strong impression of the importance of the war and an ability to visualize some of its effects, as well as a definite conviction that the Allies were in the right. If every citizen of the United States had gone through a similar experience, it is safe to say that our government would have been driven to take, certainly in 1915, and perhaps even in 1914, the step it took in 1917, so much too late.

During the first two years of his college course he pursued his studies diligently and with marked success. He was naturally shy and fastidious, making friends with youths of his own age slowly. It was easy for him to stand high in his class without strenuous work, and he had much leisure to read and think about the great subjects of human and divine government which then seemed more than ever rolled together in a bewildering confusion of prejudices, theories and scruples. Many a night when my work was done and my fire was burning low and I was wondering what dreadful news the morning papers would bring, Jack came sauntering in, with a puzzled look on his handsome face, and, throwing himself into an armchair, challenged me to conversation by asking some absurdly deep question which he knew very well I could not answer. I felt that we were helpless children, both of us, but we would often talk until the last log fell in ashes. I realised that my generation, by flinching from the problems of war and peace, of social and political reorganisation, and of religious restatement, had made victims of his generation, and that the very least we could do for them now was to be frank. The war was doing for all of us one disquieting thing: it was showing us the terrifying lack of connection between such scraps of religious conviction as we possessed and the various ideals and practices which were being brought every day into glaring prominence, ideals such as nationalism, and practices such as fighting.

Under all Jack's questioning ran a practical desire to see his own duty and find a way to perform it. His mind was settling upon a course of action. He had no fondness for military history. He had no illusions about war. He was clean and kind; he knew war was filthy and cruel. The war-fever never touched him. He was reflective and deliberate, and habitually given to looking at more than one side of any proposal. One thing was only too clear, however: this war, for the Allies and for us, was an unavoidable evil, and it had to be stopped by defeating the enemy. It was consuming the men of Britain and France. English friends he had known and loved were falling. His knowledge of life, his gratitude for the benefits of civilisation, his very gentleness would not let him rest.

In October, 1916, a few days after he was turned twenty, Jack disappeared. It was discovered presently that he had gone to Montreal, for the purpose of enlisting in the Canadian Army. His English blood had called him. Many of us, in this crisis, experienced more deeply the feeling of race and racial history and obligation than the feeling of nationality. National feeling, moreover, owing to the cruel dallying of our government, was not encouraged to express itself effectively on behalf of the Cause which was as dear to us as to any Englishman.

As the Canadian authorities were unable to accept Jack's services without his father's consent, he returned to seek it. His father pointed out to him that by entering the American Ambulance Corps in France he would be more likely to get quickly to the scene of action than in any other way; and upon this suggestion Jack at once volunteered as an ambulance driver. He filled his six months' engagement usefully, transporting, so I have been informed, at least two thousand wounded men at the French front.

On the termination of this period, in May, 1917, he endeavoured to enter the American Army without returning home; but as this was impossible, he tried to enlist in the French and then in the British Army. At this point, he came to see me at the American Ambulance Hospital in Paris, his cheeks fresh and blooming still, and the old half puzzled, half quizzical look still coming and going in his dear eyes. Legal difficulties being in the way of all his efforts, he went home and enlisted immediately in the 107th United States Infantry, of which the old 7th New York was the nucleus. A boy of twenty with a good general education and a thorough command of the French language might easily have felt justified in entering one of the students' corps for the training of officers; but Jack could not brook delay and thought that by joining a well organised old regiment as a private he would be sent to the front sooner than if he waited to obtain a commission. Through the hot summer of 1917 he was drilled in New York City, and on September thirteenth he went into camp near Spartansburg, South Carolina, with his regiment. We had our last glimpse of him at the New Year, when he came home on a short furlough. While he was in the army he was offered an opportunity to go out as an interpreter for his regiment, but he declined, not wishing to take any course easier or safer than that of a soldier in the ranks.

The 107th embarked for France in May, 1918,

and was almost at once sent into line with the rest of the Twenty-Seventh Division, on the British front, where it took part in some of the heaviest fighting of the whole war. It must have been a source of satisfaction to Jack to stand in this final crisis, shoulder to shoulder with English as well as American comrades. Nowhere between Switzerland and the sea were the Germans more firmly entrenched than they were along the Hindenburg Line. The great battle in which the Allies broke through began on the morning of September twenty-ninth. Of the one hundred and forty men of Company L, Jack's company, who went into action, only twenty-two came out alive and unwounded. He fell on the first day, at Guillemont Farm, with a bullet through his heart.

He died to make the world better. It was not hatred but love that took him into the strife, and he was one of many thousands who gave their lives, not merely for glory or for country, but because they believed it really was "a war to end war." They have handed on that task in a different form to us. Every dollar our country spends on armament should trouble our consciences; every hour that we remain outside the League of Nations should weary our patience; every lost opportunity to provide a peaceful future, in which war shall be unthought of, should lie heavy on our souls.

ACKNOWLEDGMENTS

THE ESSAYS on Scott, Coleridge, Katherine Mansfield, and George Herbert are reprinted from *The Quarterly Review,* with the kind permission of its editors.

To Belle Westcott Harper I joyously acknowledge a great debt. She suggested most of the subjects discussed in this volume, contributed any delicate touches that may be found in it, and applied to my ideas and style a kindly cruel criticism. As we were sitting in the old Nunnery garden at Christchurch, England, one sunny morning in March, 1935, she urged me to complete the series and make a book.　　　　　　　　　　　G. M. H.

CONTENTS

	PAGE
DEDICATION	v
ACKNOWLEDGMENTS	xiii
GEORGE HERBERT'S POEMS	19
THE FAMILY CORRESPONDENCE OF SIR THOMAS BROWNE	46
THE WORLD'S FIRST LOVE STORY	70
GLORIOUS SIR WALTER	89
COLERIDGE'S GREAT AND DEAR SPIRIT	103
THE MAGNANIMITY OF CHARLES LAMB	133
WORDSWORTH'S POETICAL TECHNIQUE	152
WILLIAM WATSON'S POETRY	190
KATHERINE MANSFIELD	222

LITERARY APPRECIATIONS

GEORGE HERBERT'S POEMS

Habent sua fata libelli. That books are subject to changes in taste is not always unfortunate, since by such reversals many a slumbering reputation has been revived. Modern appreciation of our seventeenth-century lyric poets, especially Donne, Wither, Carew, Habington, Herrick, Lovelace, Suckling, Herbert, Crashaw, and Vaughan, and in particular the last three, we owe in large measure to the good taste and independence of Charles Lamb and Samuel Taylor Coleridge, who broke with the literary fashion that had been high in favour since Dryden's authority began to prevail. Unfortunately, neither Lamb nor Coleridge rejected the word "metaphysical" which Samuel Johnson had fastened upon these poets, when in his *Life of Cowley* he wrote, "About the beginning of the seventeenth century appeared a race of writers that may be termed the metaphysical poets." "That, however," remarked very justly Milton's biographer, David Masson, "was a singularly unhappy choice of a name, vitiating as it did the true and specific meaning of the word 'metaphysical,' and pandering to the vulgar Georgian use of the word,

[19]

which made it an adjective for anything that seemed hard, abstract, or bewildering." Johnson's amplification of his meaning should show to any modern admirer of that "race of writers" how absurdly inapplicable the word is to them; for he goes on to say, "The metaphysical poets were men of learning, and to show their learning was their whole endeavour; but, unluckily resolving to show it in rhyme, instead of writing poetry they only wrote verses, and very often such verses as stood the trial of the finger better than of the ear; for the modulation was so imperfect that they were only found to be verses by counting the syllables." Surely this definition does not fit such inspired and highly imaginative poets as Herbert, Crashaw, and Vaughan; nor such exquisite masters of simple grace as Lovelace and Suckling; nor such resourceful and musical versifiers as Carew and Herrick. Nevertheless, "metaphysical," as applied by Johnson, has persisted. The indefatigable and omniscient but sometimes blundering and tasteless Professor Saintsbury gave it his approval; Professor Grierson used it in the title and the text of his book, *The Metaphysical Poets*. To me such use seems a misleading deflection from the proper status of a word, and no less a critical misdemeanour than the novel employment of "humanism" by the late Professor Babbitt and his school.

Attention having been, by Johnson and others, thus focussed upon complexity and fantasticality, John Donne, whose verse was the most fantastic and complex of all the seventeenth-century poets, came to be regarded, about forty years ago, as the leader and chief of men who were his superiors in the art of poetry, if not in emotional force and intellectual depth. George Herbert, Richard Crashaw, and Henry Vaughan, forsooth, have been termed his "disciples" and considered to form with him "the metaphysical school." Lecturers and teachers may be excused for talking about "schools" and "tendencies" in literature; classification simplifies their task and is easier than to communicate taste or enthusiasm for beauty. But lovers of poetry laugh at these elaborate devices, and for them every great poet is a new thing under the sun. I wish not only to protest against the misuse of the word "metaphysical," which after all is a mere detail, but to proclaim the excellence of Herbert's poetry, especially as compared with Donne's. Yet when one comes, even in a contentious mood, to the work of Herbert, that lovely structure which is indeed a temple of beauty, the spirit of controversy fades away; comparisons, distinctions, and polemics are forgotten; one is content to enjoy in peace, "kneeling in prayer, and not ashamed to pray."

Nevertheless, the stalwart figure of John Donne

is not to be passed by so easily. He was a man of powerful intellect, vast learning, and bold originality. He was the author of some passages, few and short indeed, of extremely high and rare poetic value, which blaze like fiery comets through rifts in his cloudy sky. In his poems, as in his letters and sermons, he represents, if not "the last enchantments," yet the mysterious gloom, futile ingenuity, and occasional radiance of the Middle Ages. His poems, furthermore, possess a remarkable personal interest, for they reveal not only the beauty but the foulness of a mind at once proud and devoid of reticence, filled with religious fear yet irreverent, capable both of high aspiration and of creeping cynicism. They are a confessional where the penitent is a man of immeasurable capacity, not easily understood, not lovable perhaps, formidable rather, and defying adverse judgment. His main topics are love and religion; yet he takes no pains to conceal a fierce and grotesque contempt for women, fancying himself a great scholar in that book, and he writes with gusto about putrefaction, both physical and moral, about disease and death, about deceit, envy, malice, and violence. He reports many bad smells, disgusting sights, and frightful sounds, among which last I would reckon some of his own harsh, overcrowded, and unmetrical lines. To be sure, a curious mind, with plenty of time to spare and a sufficient equipment of mediæval learning, can find diversion in puzzling out the meaning of his most intricate compositions, for example, "An Anatomie of the World."

But are such entanglements good works of art? Are they poems? Donne lacks a sense of congruity; he seldom keeps to the key or tone of his original intent; and the same is true of his versification. Ben Jonson said vivaciously: "John Donne for not keeping accent deserved hanging." He is not a successful artist, for his poetic genius is not sustained and well directed, and his poetry lacks the simplicity of great art. Though it is often passionate, this intensity of feeling almost always dissipates itself in fanciful analogies, so numerous and far-fetched as frequently to raise doubt if it be genuine. His poetry is always sensuous, often splendidly so (and, therefore, if for no other reason, not to be called metaphysical), this emphatic and varied appeal to the senses being its one strong point, apart from such interest as its puzzling intricacy arouses. It is not musical, and music is the one constant and indispensable element of good poetry. "Beauty and beauteous words should go together," as Herbert said and as he illustrated in his life and writings. Even though I consider it a blemish in Donne that the eroticism of his early life passed on into the imagery of his religious poetry, that is not the ground of my contention that he is being over-rated today. Rather it is that his verse lacks music and his thought lacks the simple beauty of good art. William Watson, with characteristic defiance of current fashion, wrote more than twenty years ago: "Neither his intellectual brilliancy and subtlety nor his prodigal wealth of fancy has saved Donne from the fate which overtakes all poets who lack the crowning grace of harmonious utterance. There are singers today who seem to cultivate a gratuitous ruggedness, forgetting that what may be effective as an exception becomes merely tedious when it constitutes the rule." Appropriate also is Coleridge's epigram "On Donne's Poetry":

> "With Donne, whose muse on dromedary trots,
> Wreathe iron pokers into true-love knots;
> Rhyme's sturdy cripple, fancy's maze and clue,
> Wit's forge and fire-blast, meaning's press and screw."

But, after all, Donne's occasional successes are very great indeed, and in fairness I must quote some of them. It was he who wrote the famous couplet:

> "No Spring nor Summer Beauty hath such grace
> As I have seen in one Autumnal face."

What an opening has his sonnet to the Earl of Dorset!—

"See, Sir, how as the Sun's hot masculine flame
Begets strange creatures on Nile's dirty slime,"

though the rest is lost in quicksands of intricacy.
One nearly perfect sonnet begins

"Deign at my hands this crown of prayer and praise,
Weav'd in my lone devout melancholy,"

and contains the pregnant phrases "my muse's
white sincerity" and "a strong sober thirst." Two
more of his Holy Sonnets, one beginning,

"At the round earth's imagined corners blow
Your trumpets, angels, and arise, arise,"

and the other,

"Death, be not proud, though some have called thee
Mighty and dreadful, for thou art not so,"

are superbly solemn. One might expect him to be
at his best in epigram, and he gives us a few good
examples:

"How great love is, presence best trial makes,
But absence tries how long this love will be;"

"Princes do in times of action get
New taxes, and remit them not in peace;"

"Be thine own palace, or the world's thy jail."

But on the whole his epigrams are wretched. If the rest of Donne's verse were equal to these passages which I have quoted, or even if there were many others of the same quality, there might be some justification for the claims that have been made for him. A powerful and original thinker he may be, but not a great poet. Let us therefore turn with higher expectation to one who has been of late somewhat obscured by the exaltation of Donne.

Though it is my chief purpose in this paper to praise the artistic qualities of George Herbert's poetry—by which I mean the music, the pictorial power, the play of imagination that make us sharers of his thought and feeling—rather than to discuss his religious convictions, something must nevertheless be said about these, for they determined the subject, tone, and imagery of his writings. Of their sincerity there can be no doubt, nor that they were the guiding principles of his life. But what kind of Christianity was this, which led its devotees to spend their days mourning for sin, alternately dreading God's wrath and curse and endeavouring to love Him, forever contemplating Christ's physical sufferings and contrasting the limitations of mortality with the glories of a life beyond the grave? Was this the religion which Christ taught? Is it not morbid? Is not its main exercise a communion between God for the one

part and a single soul for the other, disregarding
other souls and other responsibilities? Is it a religion acceptable today, one which would promote
the welfare and happiness of all mankind? Though
we may think Herbert's religion, as expressed in
his poems, too other-worldly and too much concerned with his own salvation, it is evident from
Izaak Walton's Life of him and from all else that
we know about him that he was, in spite of his
religion or because of it, a man of sweet and happy
disposition, active in good works, reasonable, sympathetic, and humane, open to the persuasions of
music and natural beauty. What did he mean by
fearing and loving God? Did he mean fearing and
loving Goodness and Truth and Beauty, or a Su-
perman with passions like our own? Perhaps he
unconsciously meant all this, and more. Perhaps
neither his nor any other poetic mind could stop
short of making God in its own image, a Being, a
Person, who includes and inspires all Goodness,
Truth, and Beauty, and therefore is to be loved
and feared and praised. Not Puritanism alone but
Catholicism too inclined this way, giving God hands
and feet, and not only Christianity, but especially
Judaism and certain so-called pagan faiths. If
Herbert's extremely anthropomorphic conception of
God seems to us childish or primitive, we may re-
flect that he was treading in the footsteps of many

a saint and prophet—and that he was a poet. To
say that mysticism is always morbid would be over-
bold. A tendency that is natural and universal and
often productive of

"Softness, and peace, and joy, and love, and bliss,"

cannot be essentially morbid. Yet Herbert's preoc-
cupation with sin and death is surely morbid. If
only men would go with open hearts and submissive
wills to the words and actions of Jesus, they would
see that the religion He taught was a way of life
summed up in the invitation to love God and our
fellow men. Sin is the negative of this positive.
To grieve endlessly for the physical suffering of
Christ was a habit of mind inherited from Catholicism and exemplified in many a mediæval picture
of the crucifixion and the descent from the cross.
To be ceaselessly tortured by doubt whether one
was really saved was a habit more characteristic of
Protestant Puritanism, especially in the seventeenth
century. The least pleasing features of Herbert's
poetry reflect these habits, which were united in
him. On the other hand his sense of fellowship with
Christ, which pervades and perfumes all his writings, was the chief source of his comfort and joy
and his grandest theme. While keeping strictly
within the bounds of orthodox theology, he brings

Christ nearer than most theologians have done,
never quite representing Him as different from or
other than God, yet conversing with Him as with a
beloved friend to whom he owed his life and all.
Many members of the Church of England, both
clergy and laity, in Herbert's time held the same
theological views and submitted themselves with
the same austerity to spiritual discipline as the dissenting Puritans. The difference in many cases was
political and ecclesiastical rather than one of religious faith. In all respects George Herbert was a
Puritan except in his regard for the historic ritual,
Episcopal ordination, and the established connection between Church and State. In him the Puritan's noble seriousness did not exclude the happy
exercise of imagination. He loved the wonders and
beauty of this material world. In his heart were
laughter and a sweet tune. Flowers in the sunshine, dew upon the grass, blue sky after rain, birds
on the wing—all these delighted him and checked a
tendency towards religious melancholy to which
he might otherwise have yielded. He was a friendly,
sympathetic pastor who had deliberately chosen a
simple life in a small country parish of poor and
uneducated people, in preference to the eminence
at court or university or in the hierarchy which his
high birth and worldly experience put within easy
reach; and though his poems contain scarcely any

references to friends or acquaintances and no narratives of human conduct, whether humble or exalted, one division of *The Temple*, namely "The Church Porch," consisting of seventy-seven stanzas, is a storehouse of maxims useful for social practice, epigrammatic observations as wise as La Rochefoucauld's, but without a trace of cynicism.

The story of Herbert's brief career, his early training in an aristocratic home, his academic triumphs at Cambridge, his renunciation of the world and retirement to the village of Bemerton, near Salisbury, his charity, his lively wit, his love of music—all this and more is treasured up for us in that little book of Lives,

> "Satellites burning in a lucid ring
> Around meek Walton's heavenly memory."

Two passages in old Izaak's best manner are so delicious that my reader, whether acquainted with them or not, might justly blame me for omitting them here. First, the young clergyman's amazing marriage:

> "His aspect was cheerful, and his speech and motion did both declare him a Gentleman; for they were all so meek and obliging that they purchased love and respect from all that knew him. These, and his

other visible virtues, begot him much love from a
Gentleman, of a Noble fortune, and a near kinsman
to his friend the Earl of Danby; namely, from Mr
Charles Danvers of Bainton, in the County of Wilts,
Esq.; this Mr Danvers having known him long and
familiarly, did so much affect him that he often and
publicly declared a desire that Mr Herbert would
marry any of his nine daughters (for he had so
many); but rather his Daughter Jane than any other,
because Jane was his beloved Daughter; And he
had often said the same to Mr Herbert himself; and
that if he could like her for a Wife, and she him for
a Husband, Jane should have a double blessing;
and Mr Danvers had so often said the like to Jane,
and so much commended Mr Herbert to her, that
Jane became so much a Platonic, as to fall in love
with Mr Herbert unseen.

"This was a fair preparation for a Marriage; but
alas, her father died before Mr Herbert's retirement
to Dauntsey; yet some friends to both parties pro-
cured their meeting; at which time a mutual affection entered into both their hearts, as a Conqueror
enters into a surprised City, and Love having got
such possession, governed and made there such
Laws and Resolutions as neither party was able to
resist; insomuch that she changed her name into
Herbert the third day after this first interview."

In the other passage Walton tells us that our
reverend and noble clergyman, walking from
Bemerton one day to "a music meeting" in Salisbury, as was his wont,

"saw a poor man with a poorer horse, that was fall-
en under his Load; they were both in distress, and
needed present help, which Mr Herbert perceiving,
put off his Canonical Coat, and helped the poor man
to unload, and after, to load his horse. . . . At his
coming to his musical friends at Salisbury, they
began to wonder that Mr George Herbert, who used
to be so trim and clean, came into that company so
soiled and discomposed; but he told them the occasion: And when one of the company told him He
had disparaged himself by so dirty an employment;
his answer was, That the thought of what he had
done would prove Music to him at Midnight; and
that the omission of it would have upbraided and
made discord in his Conscience, whensoever he
should pass by that place: For if I be bound to
pray for all that be in distress, I am sure that I am
bound, so far as it is in my power, to practise what
I pray for. And though I do not wish for the like
occasion every day, yet let me tell you, I would not
willingly pass one day of my life, without comfort-
ing a sad soul, or showing mercy; and I praise God
for this occasion. And now let us tune our instruments."

I tried at first to abridge these quotations, but
found myself in the end unwilling to break their
exquisite rhythm or lose the full flavour of their
humour, for if there are lovelier anecdotes or better told, I have yet to discover them.

Herbert's was a short but happy life, beginning
in 1593, the year when Marlowe died and Shake-

speare published *Venus and Adonis,* and ending in
1633, the year when Laud became Archbishop of
Canterbury and Milton, a young man of twenty-
four, had only recently left Cambridge and was
probably writing *Comus.* Besides his English
poems and a large amount of Latin verse, he was
the author of a collection of maxims, entitled
Jacula Prudentum, translated from foreign lan-
guages, and of a treatise entitled *A Priest to the
Temple, or the Country Parson.* This is a work in
which piety and shrewd practical sense dwell together in harmony, and which no clergyman, whatever his denomination, should neglect to read, especially if he be the shepherd of a rural flock. Its
tone is astonishingly liberal and sweet, considering
the period of ecclesiastical strife in which it was
written, just previous to the Civil War and while
the Church of England was rent with controversy.
And now let us tune our instruments!

A poet of our own day, Sir Henry Newbolt, in
his introduction to a volume of seventeenth-century
poetry, speaks incautiously of "the inferiority of
most religious verse." Then, perhaps remembering
that Dante and Milton wrote some religious verse
that was not so very inferior, he adds that by avoid-
ing what is "argumentative or abstract or historical
or theoretical," (here we must positively not steal
a glance towards Dante or Milton) "it will even

be possible for a poet to make good religious poetry." At this point, getting into still deeper water, he makes the astounding remark that "though this possibility is always with us, it has rarely brought us any but small and scattered gifts." However, the stout tomes that hold pride of place upon my shelves and in my heart refuse to shrink. The *Divina Commedia*, clear-voiced organ of a hundred pipes, seems conscious of being no small gift, and *Paradise Lost*, grandest of orchestras, knows that its harmonies are not scattered. So if one who is unacquainted with George Herbert's poetry is told that almost every line of it is religious, one need not expect to find it for that reason inferior. There is indeed a considerable proportion of it, possibly a third, which is excessively intricate and far-fetched, or trivial in substance, or tediously iterative. Herbert's gifts are scattered, it is true, but they are not small. Like Donne, but to a far less extent, he lacks architectonic skill; for though the body of his work is called *The Temple*, its unity is to be found rather in the spirit of the designer than in the structure he has built. He has brought to one field many blocks of coloured marble, but has not set half of them in place. After all, however, ability to erect vast artistic fanes or pleasure-domes is exceedingly rare, and in Herbert's workyard, as in those of most poets, we must be content to enjoy the beautiful marble blocks.

In default of the great temple, let us build a little chapel with the finest grained and most highly polished of these, or rather with pieces of them, for want of space forbids long quotations. As head of the corner I choose two stanzas from "The Flower," which seems to me the loveliest of Herbert's poems. After one of those seasons of dejection to which some of the most ardent religious natures are subject, he feels once more the sunshine of God's favour, and sings:

> "Who would have thought my shrivel'd heart
> Could have recover'd greenness? It was gone
>   Quite under ground; as flowers depart
> To see their mother-root, when they have blown,
>   Where they together
>   All the hard weather,
> Dead to the world, keep house unknown.
>
> "And now in age I bud again,
> After so many deaths I live and write;
>   I once more smell the dew and rain,
> And relish versing: O, my only Light,
>   It cannot be
>   That I am he
> On whom Thy tempests fell at night."

In John Donne's "Hymn to Christ" occur the following lines:

> "As the tree's sap doth seek the root below
> In winter, in my winter now I go,
> Where none but thee, th' Eternal root
> Of true Love I may know;"

but even if Herbert had seen them, which is by no means certain, he gave the idea a lovelier and more developed form. His entire poem, of six stanzas, is full of joy, like a child who, sweet and clean, goes forth to play in the spring sunshine.

The poem "Easter," beginning "Rise, heart, thy Lord is risen; sing His praise," is in the same happy strain, and holds a wonderful surprise, when the long lines, somewhat complicated in meaning, give way to a song, in the simplest of metres, beginning:

> "I got me flowers to straw Thy way,
> I got me boughs off many a tree;
> But Thou wast up by break of day
> And brought'st Thy sweets along with Thee."

The short, quick swing of these lines suggests the confident stride of one who has taken fresh heart of hope and goes forth in cheerful mood upon a sunshine holiday. His thought runs constantly upon music. Prayer with him is "a kind of tune":

"Softness, and peace, and joy, and love, and bliss,
Exalted manna, gladness of the best,
Heaven in ordinary, man well drest,
The milky way, the bird of Paradise,
Church-bells beyond the stars heard, the soul's blood,
The land of spices, something understood."

This heaping up of metaphors is characteristic of his genius. It also marks and sometimes mars the genius of his age. We find it in the writings of almost all his contemporaries and down through the second and third quarters of the century, not only in poetry but in imaginative prose, for example in Sir Thomas Browne's *Religio Medici*. Milton's concentration of purpose and no doubt also his severe classical training forbade him the excessive indulgence of fancy; this difference between him and the minor poets illustrating well Coleridge's distinction between that faculty and imagination. But let not the number and variety of metaphors in this extract from Herbert's poem on Prayer prevent our enjoyment of their individual beauty. Let them dwell in our memory like strains of music, suggestions of immortal longings, "something understood" but not to be fully expressed, something that passes the bounds of time and space, "church-bells beyond the stars heard."

The Puritan respect for Sunday, as a continuation and consecration of the Hebrew Sabbath, may seem hard to explain historically or justify on grounds of reason. That it was often overdone few would now deny. The Church of England, making Sunday a time neither of riotous pleasure nor of penitential gloom, deserves credit for having held a middle course between worldly disregard and the superstitious, burdensome observance practiced by Scottish and dissenting Christians. Herbert's poem "Sunday" is in the liberal Anglican vein, and, beginning with reverent cheerfulness,

> "O Day most calm, most bright,
> The fruit of this, the next world's bud,"

goes on through a series of comparisons, some of them nobly plain, others quite fantastic, to a climax which must have shocked some readers and may do so still—"Thou art a day of mirth." Many of Herbert's poems are cries of religious ecstasy, either contrite or triumphant. Few of them express despair or the torture of a soul that is in doubt whether it may not after all be eternally damned, a state of mind not uncommon among Calvinists of his day and of the eighteenth century. Anyone who has had the great good fortune to read David Brainerd's Diary, edited by Jonathan Edwards, will recall his agonising fear lest he might be indulging in "carnal security" and his outcry, "Alas! all my

good frames were but self-righteousness, not
founded on a desire for the glory of God." This
world was to Brainerd what a railway junction
might be to a man who had gone there to meet the
woman he loved, not a place interesting for its own
sake. Passion sometimes transfigures circumstances, sometimes obliterates them. Herbert being
less other-worldly than the American saint, his religious passion finds new splendour in the sun and
lends fresh colour to the rose, making "the too
much loved Earth more lovely." He counts up the
agencies that serve us: the trees bear us fruit, the
winds blow for us,

> "The stars have us to bed,
> Night draws the curtain, which the sun withdraws;
> Music and light attend our head;"

and concludes with a prayer:

> "Since then, my God, Thou hast
> So brave a palace built, O dwell in it,
> That it may dwell with Thee at last!
> Till then afford us so much wit
> That, as the world serves us, we may serve Thee,
> And both Thy servants be."

Yet, for all this exaltation, he does not neglect to
apply his religion to the affairs of daily life, as may

be seen not only in the comparatively secular poem
"The Church Porch," which is composed largely of
practical maxims, but also in the well-known lines
from "The Elixir":

> "Teach me, my God and King,
>   In all things Thee to see,
> And what I do in anything
>   To do it as for Thee.
>
> "A servant with this clause
>   Makes drudgery divine;
> Who sweeps a room as for thy laws
>   Makes that and th' action fine."

I care far more for the simple and natural beauties
that abound in Herbert than for his conceits, however quaint; but there is one stanza that contains
comparisons so amusing that I am fain to quote it.
The lines occur in an address to Divine Providence,
the orderliness of whose ways he has been praising:

> "To show Thou are not bound, as if Thy lot
> Were worse than ours, sometimes Thou shiftest hands:
> Most things move th' under-jaw, the crocodile not;
> Most things sleep lying, th' elephant leans or stands."

Sir Thomas Browne, being a physician, was less
inclined to accept the vulgar error that an elephant has no joints, and took pains to refute it.

Having escaped close contact with the crocodile, I cannot say which jaw it moves.

Let it not be supposed, however, that the main theme of Herbert's muse was not redemption from sin through the sacrifice of Christ. He is conscious of his own sinful nature, besides admitting his relationship to Adam, yet never for a moment loses sight of God's mercy. This twofold sense is perhaps best shown in the richly laden poem beginning "Lord, with what care hast Thou begirt us round":

> "Pulpits and Sundays, sorrow dogging sin,
> Afflictions sorted, anguish of all sizes,
> Fine nets and stratagems to take us in,
> Bibles laid open, millions of surprises;
>
> "Blessings beforehand, ties of gratefulness,
> The sound of glory ringing in our ears,
> Without, our shame; within, our consciences;
> Angels and grace, eternal hopes and fears.
>
> "Yet all these fences and their whole array
> One cunning bosom sin blows all away."

Contrition and a sense of danger are voiced in other poems, and with them a struggle to resist God's offer of salvation and find out some other way. Then, in the midst of a protest, "My lines and life are free; free as the road, Loose as the wind," there comes a sudden change:

"But as I raved and grew more fierce and wild
  At every word,
Methought I heard one calling 'Child';
  And I replied 'My Lord.' "

Thenceforth there is no turning back nor any thought of doing so. He goes whither he is led, and with relief he sings:

"Whereas my birth and spirit rather took
  The way that takes the town,
Thou didst betray me to a lingering book
  And wrap me in a gown."

Filled with a restless desire to serve his new Master, he cries:

"Now I am here, what Thou wilt do with me
  None of my books will show:
I read and sigh, and wish I were a tree,—
  For sure then I would grow
To fruit or shade; at least some bird would trust
  Her household to me, and I should be just,"

And again:

"All things are busy; only I
  Neither bring honey with the bees,
Nor flowers to make that, nor the husbandry
  To water these."

There is either a remarkable coincidence or a deeper and very interesting connection between a certain phrase of Herbert's and a much discussed passage in Milton's *Comus*. It occurs in the poem entitled "Faith." Herbert sings, "There is a rare outlandish root, which when I could not get, I found it here," meaning apparently in faith, while "outlandish," of course, has its usual seventeenth-century significance of "foreign." The Attendant Spirit in *Comus* speaks of "a small unsightly root, But of divine effect," which "in another country . . . Bore a bright golden flower, but not in this soil." *Comus* was performed in 1634 at Ludlow Castle, not far from the ancestral home of the Herberts, in Montgomeryshire. George Herbert's poems were first printed in 1633.

Short extracts, a few lines here and there, and even single phrases, show Herbert's felicitous qualities better than long ones, and no entire poem is altogether free from blemish—a strained conceit, an incongruous juxtaposition of ideas, or a false rhyme. One of the pleasures of reading him is looking out for the flashes of inspiration, the nuggets of pure gold. To take only one more example: in an otherwise not very successful poem occurs the line, "What is so shrill as silent tears?"

Scant justice has been done to Herbert in any anthology of English verse with which I am acquainted, and it is this fact that has led me to write this essay. The anthologists, apparently accepting the time-worn classification of him as a disciple of Donne and a "metaphysical" poet, and accepting also Doctor Johnson's arbitrary definition of "metaphysical," have culled out his extravagant conceits and printed them in preference to his real beauties, which are natural and simple. Of a quite different kind from his purely religious poems are the stanzas called "The Church Porch," a large collection of maxims, many of them wise and witty, as a handful may suffice to show. Here is one which may have furnished Walt Whitman with a famous phrase:

> "By all means use sometimes to be alone;
>   Salute thyself."

In defense of a strictly regulated life he says:

> "Entice the trusty sun, if that you can,
> From his ecliptic line; beckon the sky!
> Who lives by rule, then, keeps good company."

Better known are these:

> "A verse may find him who a sermon flies,
> And turn delight into a sacrifice."

> "Kneeling ne'er spoiled silk stocking."

And there is no better rule for a hostess who wishes to encourage conversation and make her guests happy than the following:

> "Entice all neatly to what they know best;
> For so thou dost thyself and him a pleasure,"

and no better counsel for one whose pleasant task is like this of mine, than Herbert's advice to scholars: "Copy fair what Time hath blurred."

THE FAMILY CORRESPONDENCE OF
SIR THOMAS BROWNE

THERE exists a rich treasury of human affection and intelligence that has seldom been explored and is now open only to those who have access to an expensive and rare work published in 1836, namely *Sir Thomas Browne's Works, Including His Life and Correspondence,* edited by Simon Wilkin in four volumes, or to an abbreviated reproduction of the same in Bohn's Antiquarian Library, 1852. Browne's own letters, but not those he received, were published in 1931, more fully and correctly than by Wilkin, in the sixth volume of Mr. Geoffrey Keynes' scholarly edition. In the letters that passed between the author of *Religio Medici* and his two sons, Edward and "honest Tom," we gain admittance to a domestic circle which can scarcely have had many equals for sweetness and light in any part of the world or any age. If to the culture of the younger Pliny, whom I conceive to have represented the highest refinement of Roman society, we add the glory of Christian humility and Christian kindness, we may rightly estimate this seventeenth-century English family.

There are several excellent Lives of the famous physician and author, and to enumerate the editions of his works, both in English and in translations, might exhaust the patience of a candidate for academic honours. Dr. William Osler showed me, in 1907, his immense collection of the *Religio Medici,* which, if I remember correctly, covered the walls of a whole room in his house at Oxford. It is still one of the most vital books of that century, so rich in great and enduring prose works, being, I fancy, read voluntarily and for pleasure more than any other of them except the Authorized Version of the Bible, Bacon's *Essays, The Compleat Angler,* and *Pilgrim's Progress,* though this front rank is hard pressed, for quality but not for general interest, by Walton's *Lives,* Milton's *Areopagitica,* Jeremy Taylor's *Holy Living* and *Holy Dying,* and George Herbert's *Country Parson.*

Much less popular, and indeed less worthy of liking, yet by no means negligible if only for one glorious sentence which it contains, is Browne's *Hydriotaphia: Urn Burial; or a Discourse of the Sepulchral Urns lately found in Norfolk.* Who has not heard of the bones that have "quietly rested under the drums and tramplings of three conquests"? What startling imagery! What hypnotic rhythm! *The Garden of Cyrus, or the Quincuncial, Lozenge, or Net-work Plantations of the Ancients,*

Artificially, Naturally, Mystically Considered, is too fantastic, too mediæval, too uselessly learned for most readers in our time. The *Pseudodoxia Epidemica, or Enquiries into Vulgar Errors,* though it must appear to practical people mere elaborate trifling, is amusing, and not without value for the light it throws on the capacity of the human mind to believe the incredible. To behold Doctor Browne destroy a once popular delusion that elephants have no joints does not add to our knowledge of the elephant, but it contributes to our understanding of man. Next to *Religio Medici* in splendour of language and in wisdom is Browne's *Christian Morals,* published after his death, a treatise running over with quotable passages; for example: "Be charitable before wealth make thee covetous, and lose not the glory of the mite"; "Live by old ethics and the classical rules of honesty"; "Think not that morality is ambulatory, that vices in one age are not vices in another"; "Be substantially great in thyself, and more than thou appearest unto others; and let the world be deceived in thee, as they are in the lights of heaven"; "When thou lookest upon the imperfections of others, allow one eye for what is laudable in them."

If one knew nothing more of Browne than is revealed in *Religio Medici, Pseudodoxia Epidemica, Hydriotaphia,* and *The Garden of Cyrus,* one might think of him as the very embodiment of mediævalism, credulous, mystical, dependent upon authority, and using the evidence of his senses to confirm rather than to test ancient opinion. But a new spirit was awake in England, Holland, and France, and also, despite the Thirty Years' War, in Central Europe. Everybody that discovers by trial and error how to perform acts not purely automatic is employing the inductive method of research; but Bacon and Descartes had defined it and proclaimed its value as the Novum Organum or appropriate instrument for scientific inquiry and the advancement of learning. *Ibi incipit vita nova.* At this point modern times begin. Four dates are very significant: Bacon died in 1626, Kepler in 1630, Descartes in 1650, and the Royal Society of London for improving Natural Knowledge was incorporated in 1662. Though the seventeenth century was one of religious and political strife, as most centuries are, there were periods of calm in which the investigation of facts went quietly on and free speculation was unimpeded by bigotry or national prejudice. In England as contrasted with France there were then and still are many important intellectual centres besides the capital. Norwich was one of these. Physicians, by the nature of their profession, are or should be observant of phenomena, able to rise above routine, willing to reject rules that do not work, and curious about the infinite variety of discoverable facts. In the life of our Norwich physician we can observe the triumph of inductive logic over mediæval modes of thought, the conflict, by no means decisive either then or now, between faith and reason, the hospitality to new ideas, and the reliance upon experiment which characterise the modern world. He is an outstanding example of what the Renaissance accomplished, for the process was after all a return to Greek methods and he had the universal curiosity and critical habit of an Aristotle. We might perhaps perceive this representative character of his even in the five treatises I have mentioned; yet the mediæval aspect would be more striking. In his correspondence, however, the modern side appears definitely and emphatically.

Interesting and important as Browne could be shown to be in this general way, as representing the change from one great era to another, it is to a humbler task that I address myself, namely to describe his domestic correspondence, chiefly with his two sons, though glancing now and then at a few letters and postscripts written to or by other members of the family. In Wilkin's collection there are one hundred and five letters from the father to his elder son Edward, forty-nine from Edward to him, fifteen from the father to the younger son Tom, six from Tom to him, one from the father to both boys, two to Tom from his mother, two from Edward to one of his sisters, two from Edward to Tom, one from Edward to his mother, and about thirty short notes and postscripts from the mother to various members of the family and from the father to his daughters and daughter-in-law.

Browne was born in London in 1605, received his academic education at Winchester and Oxford, studied medicine at Montpellier, Padua and Leyden, settled as a physician in the East Anglian city of Norwich, prospered greatly in his profession, wrote *Religio Medici* when he was about thirty years old and his other books in quick succession, married an excellent woman, had two sons and several daughters, rose to such eminence in his own town that in 1671 he was knighted by King Charles II as its most distinguished citizen, and died, full of honours after a useful and happy life, in 1682. The only departure from rational and humane conduct recorded against him is that in the trial of two women accused of witchcraft he testified his belief in that horrible superstition. His wife Dorothy was a good mother and grandmother, with more sense than education. Her orthography is delightfully original and constitutes part of the charm of the postscripts in which she reports the doings of her grandson Tommy to his mother, Edward's wife, in London, as may be seen in the following example: "Deare Daughter, I thanck God for your latter, and shall be so glad to see my Tomey returne in helth though ever so durty. He knows fullars earth will cleane all. I besich God of his mercy blesse you all. Your affectinat Mothar, Dorothy Browne." Little Tommy spent much of his boyhood with his grandparents in Norwich.

The elder son, Edward, was born about 1643, studied at Cambridge and Oxford, travelled extensively, and from his father's point of view expensively, on the Continent, going even into the Balkan countries, practiced medicine in London, and became a member of the Royal Society, devoting much of his time to biological research, till his death, in 1708. The younger son, Thomas, was born in 1647, travelled abroad in his turn, entered the Navy in 1664, conducted himself gallantly and humanely in the wars with France and Holland, and died about 1667.

To some readers it may be surprising, to all it must be gratifying, to learn from their correspondence on what a high plane of culture this middle-class English family lived, three centuries ago. Though provincial, being associated more with Norfolk than with the metropolis, and always retaining an interest in local affairs, they were also Europeans in their outlook, and among them at one time or another the men visited almost every country between the English Channel and the Black Sea. In the midst of political storms, civil war, and theological strife, they preserved in their souls a place of calm retreat, wherein to carry on intellectual activity, neighbourly amenity, "the fair humanities of old religion." Community of interests made them acquainted with some of the nobility and some high ecclesiastics, but they remained on the whole associated with people of their own class or their own scientific pursuits.

Another and more important source of interest is the intense intellectual curiosity the letters disclose. This curiosity concerned literary and historical matters, but chiefly the secrets of nature. There was no branch of natural science about which the two physicians were not well informed and keenly eager to learn the latest discoveries. An eclipse of the sun meant more to them than the extinction of a kingdom. The appearance of a comet set their minds ablaze and brought them into correspondence with astronomers in remote parts of the world. The arrival of a live ostrich in England occasioned a brisk interchange of letters between London and Norwich, which ended only when Edward finally appeased his burning desire to dissect the bird. Minerals in Bohemia and Hungary, fishes in the Danube, strange plants in Germany and Italy, diseases old and new, with symptoms rare and remedies hope-inspiring, are reported and discussed. I know not whether the seventeen-year locust exists outside my own country, but if the Brownes had witnessed its emergence as a dusty miner from symmetrical holes in the earth, its un-erring crawl to the nearest tree, whereon to break loose from its armor and goggles, its weak and soft appearance for the first hour thereafter, its trium-phant achievement of the art of aviation on glisten-ing wings, the shrill peal of the male as he causes the concertina under his wings to vibrate, the mat-ing of the sexes, the scoring of twigs and deposition of eggs by the female, the fall of these twigs to the ground, and then, mysterious sixteen years and ten months of subterranean existence, under what sys-tem of political economy or what social order no man knoweth—if those two ardent investigators had seen and heard the seventeen-year locust, what would have been their excitement and how many more letters they would have written! Had I ven-tured to write a history of the cryptic phase of the locust's cycle, I am sure I should have earned Doctor Johnson's condemnatory remark that "it is a perpetual triumph of fancy to expand a scanty theme, to raise glittering ideas from obscure prop-erties, and to produce to the world an object of wonder to which nature had contributed little." But the Brownes were men of science.

Last, but not least, the correspondence reassures us in regard to the home life of our ancestors, for it discloses the sweet intimacies of a kindly, gentle, open-minded family, devoted to good works, highly civilised, and religious without bigotry. It had taken many centuries to develop such a family and the environment favourable to its growth. One likes to think, and probably is right in thinking, that there were hundreds similar to it, not only in England, but in many other countries. However that may be, here was one at least. To contemplate its virtues may cure us of the all too natural assumption that we modern people are the crown of creation and the fine flower of all time.

Now for some extracts from the letters. When the second son, Thomas, or "honest Tom" as his father calls him, was about fourteen years old he was sent abroad to see the world and learn manners. "I hope by God's assistance you have been some weeks in Bourdeaux," writes his father. "Hold fast to the Protestant Religion and be diligent in going to church when you have any little knowledge of the language. . . . View and understand all notable buildings and places in Bourdeaux or near it, and take a draught thereof, as also the ruind Amphitheatre. . . . Read some books of french and latin, for I would by no means you should loose your latin but rather gain more." "Take notice of all things remarkable, which will be pleasant unto you hereafter. . . . I would be glad you had a good handsome garb of your body, which you will observe in most there, and may quickly learn if you cast off *pudor rusticus,* and take up a commendable boldness without which you will never be fit for anything nor able to show the good parts which God has given you. . . . Good boy doe not trouble thy self to send us any thing, either wine or bacon." Under date of April 22, 1661, he writes: "There are great preparitions against to-morrow, the Coronation day . . . long and solemn service at Christ Church beginning at 8 a clock and with a sermon ending at twelve, . . . speeches and a little play by the strollers in the market place, an other by young Cityzens at Timber Hill on a stage, Cromwell hangd and burnt every where, whose head is now upon Westminster hall, together with Ireton and Bradshows. Have the love and fear of God ever before thine eyes: God confirm your faith in Christ and that you may live accordingly. Je vous recommende a Dieu. If you meet any pretty insects of any kind keep them in a box."

Perhaps by this time the gentle doctor would be reconciled to behold the statue of Cromwell which now stands, an object of honour, not many paces from the spot where his head was once exposed to public scorn.

In another letter he again alludes to Tom's English bashfulness, as in the following sentence: "Be temperate and sober in the whole course of your life, keep noe bad or uncivill company be courteous and humble in your Conversation still shunning *pudor rusticus,* which undoes good natures, and practise an handsome garb and civil boldness which he that learneth not in France travaileth in vain. Gods Blessing be upon you. I rest your ever Loveing father, Tho. Browne." He keeps the boy informed of the great events in London which followed the Restoration, and also of local politics in Norfolk, the sermons preached in Norwich cathedral, and the price of wheat.

Tom's narrative of his journey from Bordeaux to Paris shows that he had profited by his father's advice to keep his eyes open for notable buildings and antiquities. His observations show uncommon intelligence in so young a lad. A longer journal of a tour with his brother soon afterwards in Derbyshire and other midland counties may have been written by either of the boys. It abounds in lively remarks on men and things, shows the family trait of scientific curiosity, and is a jolly piece of youthful composition. The climax comes when they catch sight of home and their hearts swell with local pride: "When towards night, recollecting and discoursing of all the citys and places wee had mette with in this our little more than fortnight's

journey, to consummate all, that famous city of
Norwich presents itself to our view; Christ Church
high spire, the old famous castle, eight and thirty
goodly churches, the fields about it and the stately
gardens in it, did so lessen our opinion of any wee
had seen, that it seem'd to us to deride our rambling folly."

Tom was inclined to literature as well as to ar-
chæology and architecture, and as a junior naval
officer, in a letter to his father reporting the con-
voying of merchantmen and the capture of prizes,
he says: "I lately read a good part of Lucan,
whose sentences, orations, and noble straynes I like
very well; and to say truth, some other poets of
great name seeme to me butt flat in comparison of
him." This pleased the parent, who replied in a
long and very affectionate letter, urging him not to
follow ancient examples of suicidal heroism in
case he were captured: "To be made prisoner by
an unequall and overruling power, after a due re-
sistance, is no disparagement. . . . God hath given
you a stout, but a mercifull heart withall; and in all
your life you could never behold any person in
miserie butt with compassion and relief; which hath
been notable in you from a child: so have you layd
up a good foundation for God's mercy; and if such
a disaster should happen, Hee will, without doubt,
mercifully remember you."

Of practical advice to both sons there is no lack, and it is always reasonable and wise, as for example this to Edward: "Hazard not your own health by any intemperance with H. F., for men who must have drinck and company are content with any, and are litle obliged by compliance or joynt intemperance, at least it is soon forgott, and tis the greatest friendship that can be testified to dehort them from excesse, which destroyes themselves at last, and their children before."

The published correspondence between Sir Thomas and his son Edward, who after prolonged study and travel practiced medicine with great success in London, covers the years from 1664 to 1682, and is a record not only of paternal and filial affection, but of a common interest in professional matters and all kinds of scientific inquiry. The scientific spirit showed itself early in Edward. In his diary when he was quite young occur such entries as "Cutting up a turkey's heart," "We got a hare's bladder," "I boyled the right forefoot of a munkey, and took out all the bones, which I keep by mee." Sir Thomas constantly helped him by sending him medical prescriptions, advice about surgical methods, and material for his lectures. He also counselled him frequently to be temperate and to take sufficient recreation. Who has not known at least one overworked doctor whose life might have been prolonged had he taken the elder Browne's advice to his son: "Extraordinarie sickly seasons woorrie physitians, and robb them of their health as well as their quiet; have therefore a great care of your health, and order your affayres to the best preservation thereof which may bee by temperance, and sobrietie, and a good competence of sleepe. Take heed that tobacco gayne not to much upon you, for the great incommodities that may ensue, and the bewiching qualitie of it, which drawes a man to take more and more the longer hee hath taken it." To the letter from which this passage is taken Dame Dorothy adds a postscript, saying: "I give you and my good daughter many thankes for your great kindness to your sisters. They are very sensable of it, and Tomey very much ashamed that he behaved himself no better, but hopps hee shall the next time. He is now as sivell as I can wish him, and spends much of his time with grandfather."

In a postscript about a year later she reports: "He is now a very good boy for his boak, I can assuer you, and delights to read to his grandfather and I, when he coms from schole." The grandfather writes: "Tom holds well, though he toyles and moyles at all sorts of play and after school. Wee take all care we can to make him sitt still and spare himself and to bee a litle more composed and attentive to instructions and learne, and do all wee can to have sober stayd litle girles for his play-fellowes that hee maie imitate them." And again: "I have been fayne to hire him to sitt still half an hower." Tranquillity and equanimity this wise doctor considered to be the very foundation stones of well-being, and he had long before written to Edward when the latter was abroad, in 1669, "Though your body be in motion, maintaine a tranquillitie and smoothnesse of mind, which will better conserve your health." Before we say good-by to Tommy, here is a sentence by his grand-father which is sadly touching when we remember that the boy's Uncle Tom had died long before: "The fayrings were wellcome to Tom, hee finds about the howse divers things that were your brothers, and Betty sometimes tells him stories about him, so that hee was importunate with her to write his life in a quarter of a sheet of paper and read it unto him, and will have still some more added." Again he writes: "The players are at the Red Lyon, hard by, and Tom goes sometimes to see a playe." It is amusing to find that the learned author was almost as weak in punctuation and spelling as Mistress Dorothy his wife, especially when he exhorts Tomey to "remember to make comas, as (,) and full points at the end of a sentence thus (.)"

He urges the busy London doctor to keep up his reading of the ancient classics: "It were good to read some of the Latin poets sometimes, because they are known to so many, and have handsome expressions and sense. . . . Your brother Thomas, when hee was at sea, learned much of Horace and all Juvenal in a manner without booke."

A letter from Sir Thomas to his daughter, Mrs. Lyttleton, contains a passage in the style of *Religio Medici;* it begins: "Some wear away in calmes, some are caried away in storms: we come into the world one way, there are many gates to goe out of it." Between a passage on anatomy and one on the smallpox he injects a wise and clement remark: "Some imperfections will bee found in the best authors, and most excusable in them who lesse accuse or find fault with others." It is impossible to get away from "litle Tomey," and we have a pleasant glimpse of family life when his grandfather, *à propos* of cider, writes to Edward: "My wife and others, except myself, drinck a little at meales; and Tom calls for the bottomes of the glasses, where tis sweetest, and cares litle for the rest."

Edward had some thought of making a new translation of *Plutarch's Lives,* and upon this congenial topic his father dilated at considerable length, remarking shrewdly that "if the disused

words and some other faults had been altered,
North's translation might have suffised and still
passed, especially with gentlemen, who, if the expression bee playne looke not into criticismes,"—
which confirms an opinion I long since acquired,
that pedants are not always gentlemen.

Again that irrepressible youngster pops up:
"Your Tomey grows a stout fellow, I hope you
will com and see him this summer, hee is in great
expextion of a tumbler you must send him for his
popet show, a punch he has and his wife, and a
straw king and quen, and ladies of honor, and all
things but a tumbler, which this town cannot aford:
it is a wodin fellow that turns his heles over his
head."

Sir Thomas prophesied truly when he wrote to
Edward: "I doubt the English will not like the
setting up of a colledge of physitians in Scotland. . . . If they sett up a colledge and breed many
physitians, wee shall bee sure to have a great part
of them in England."

He advises Edward to lay aside his habitual
modesty and speak loud and clearly when lecturing.
He was much pleased to transmit to him a message from another physician, an old friend, who
said, "You performed your publick lectures so
much like a gentleman and with so much learning
as had not been done for these 7 and 7 yeares."

Though Edward's practice was profitable, he was not to count upon its being always so: "Now is your time to be frugall and lay up. I thought myself rich enough till my children grew up. . . . Excesse in apparell and chargeable dresses are got into the country, especially among woemen; men go decently and playn enough." In reference to a repulsive practice which is not uncommon in certain quarters today, he remarks with amusement or repugnance: "The Turks and Eastern nations paynt their nayles of a reddish colour, . . . and sometimes the maines and tayles of their horses."

Far more numerous than the bits of family news, the exhortations to right living, and the expressions of affection are the remarks on scientific discoveries and problems, especially in the field of medicine and surgery. Samuel Johnson, in his *Life of Sir Thomas Browne*, exhibits his characteristic scorn for what he does not understand by scoffing at Edward's universal interest, saying that he was "by the train of his studies, led to enquire most after those things by which the greatest part of mankind is little affected; a great part of his book [Edward Browne's narrative of his travels] seems to contain very unimportant accounts of his passage from one place where he saw little to another where he saw no more." But this need not affect our judgment of Edward Browne's gifts, for Johnson's criticism of Sir Thomas's literary style is equally illiberal: "It is vigorous, but rugged; it is learned, but pedantick; it is deep, but obscure; it strikes, but does not please; it commands, but does not allure: his tropes are harsh, and his combinations uncouth." Here the eighteenth century sits in judgment on the seventeenth, convention on originality, dullness on humour, security on adventure.

Sir Thomas, in a letter to his son, expresses doubt whether "there bee thirteen thousand millions of men upon the whole earth," meaning perhaps one hundred thousand by "million," in which case he would have been not far wrong. He refers to speculations about "a flying man, and a shippe to sayle in the ayre." Again he writes: "I took notice this weeke of the notable voyce of a hound above all other doggs; and therefore at your opportunity you may examine the vocall organs of a hound; there may be something considerable, perhaps, beside the rest, from the frame of his mouth and slabbing lipps." He suggests that Edward should examine a report of "a person borne deaf, who could heare if they shaved his head upon the coronall suture, and washed it cleane, and then one put his mouth to it and spoke." Recent experiments have proved that the deaf can be made to hear by vibrations of the skull. The skull was a favourite topic, and he writes a few weeks later: "I sent unto you

the skull of a poulcat's head. . . . I gave a badger's
skull unto Dr. Clarke, and if you meet with an
opportunity, keep one."

The subject of greatest interest was the arrival
of several ostriches in England. From the context
in which this earth-shattering event is first mentioned, I judge they were brought as a present to
King Charles by the ambassador of the King of
Fez and Morocco. The ostrich was regarded not
only as a rare zoölogical wonder, but as a pharma-
ceutical treasure. Highly as I value the civilisation
of seventeenth-century England, I am glad we do
not have to take some of the medicines prescribed
by even the most enlightened physicians of that
time. Writing of the London ostriches, Sir Thomas
remarks: "If any of them dye, I beleeve it will
bee dissected; they have odde feet and strong
thighes and legges. Tis much the use of the
eggeshells is not more common in physick, like
other eggeshells and crabbs eyes or clawes; and
there would be enough to bee had, if they were
looked after, and sought for, by the droggesters.
Perhaps the king will putt 3 or 4 of these oestridges
into St. James' park, and give away the rest to some
noblemen." But what joy! Edward himself obtained one of the birds; and his father in a long
letter written only a few months before he died
gives minute directions for feeding it, keeping it

warm, and in the sad event of its demise, dissecting it: "I beleeve you must bee careful of your oestridge, this return of cold wether, least it perish by being bredd in so hot a country, and perhaps not seen snowe before or very seldome, so that I beleeve it must be kept under covert, and have strawe to sitt upon, and water sett by it to take of, both day and night. . . . If you give any iron it may be wrapped up in doue or past; perhaps it will not take it up alone. You may trie whether it will eat a worme, or a very small eele." He promises to send his son the works of Aldrovandus, Johnstonus, Bellonius, and some others, in which ostriches are depicted or described, and contributes further information from the works of Ray, Nierembergius, and Willoughby.

Another and no less serious topic was malaria, which under the names of quartan, tertian, double quartan, and double tertian fever, was very prevalent in Norfolk, probably because of the extensive fens in that county. Some of the remedies mentioned seem fantastic and even noxious, especially bleeding and the opening of "issues" or running sores to permit the expulsion of evil "humours"; but Sir Thomas wisely, as time went on, became more and more inclined to prescribe what he calls *cortex*, which doubtless was Peruvian bark, *i. e.*, quinine.

Though the letters contain many references to

politics, they are noticeably free from expressions of political prejudice, fear, or tension. The Brownes were royalists and Anglicans, but apparently without antipathy for republicans and dissenters. They lived through a period of civil, and another of foreign, war, yet nothing seems to have shaken their sense of security.

Unfortunately we possess very few letters from Sir Thomas to his daughters. One of them, Mrs. Lyttleton, lived in the island of Guernsey, and to her he wrote, a short time before his death: "When I travailed beyond sea I resolved to my best power to doe nothing which should trouble my mind when I returned into my own country. I know you will indeavour to do the like."

When we turn from what is merely temporary and incidental to qualities eternal and universal, we find in this correspondence a precious residue of sweet and happy things: family love and loyalty and helpfulness, particularly between father and son. It would be difficult to decide whether the solicitude of the father exceeds the filial pride and respect of the sons. The affection is mutual; all have the same interests, the same high ideals of conduct, and especially the same constant desire to be useful to their fellow men. All were good citizens of the world, with an outlook far wider and nobler than mere nationalism. All were alert, open-

minded, public-spirited, progressive, devout. Each
of them illustrates a passage of justifiable bravery
in *Christian Morals:* "Bright Thoughts, Clear
Deeds, Constancy, Fidelity, Bounty, and generous
Honesty are the gems of noble Minds; wherein, to
derogate from none, the true Heroick English Gentleman hath no Peer."

THE WORLD'S FIRST LOVE STORY

"As one who, long in populous city pent,
Where houses thick and sewers annoy the air,
Forth issuing on a summer's morn, to breathe
Among the pleasant villages and farms
Adjoined, from each thing met conceives delight—
The smell of grain, or tedded grass, or kine,
Or dairy, each rural sight, each rural sound—
If chance with nymph-like step fair virgin pass,
What pleasing seemed for her now pleases more,
She most, and in her look sums all delight."

WITH these lines from the Ninth Book of *Paradise Lost* as my text, I propose to show that Milton wrote the world's first love story. It is the *first* love story because its theme is the love of the first man and the first woman, and also because it is, as Milton tells it, the most beautiful, most touching, most tragic, and most representative. It is unmatched in classic myth or poesy, or in mediæval romances of chivalry, or in Dante, Chaucer, or Shakespeare, or in modern fiction. One of its threads of interest appears again, though twisted almost beyond recognition, in Tolstoi's *Resurrection*, but without the splendour of Milton's imagery and the magic of his music. Thackeray too, in *Henry Esmond,* which I dare to name the greatest English novel, describes the mystery of a woman's charm and a man's recognition of *i segni dell' antica fiamma;* but prose is prose and poetry is poetry.

To call Milton the greatest celebrant of female beauty and fascination, the most seductive painter of amorous delights, the most candid acknowledger of woman's power to mould the destiny of man, may seem amazing, and most readers of such a statement will be reluctant to accept it without proof.

The reluctance is due in part to the hostility which many persons bear towards Milton on account of his political opinions and affiliations. They entertain, after all these years, a romantic attachment to King Charles I, whom they regard as a martyr. Monarchy to them is a sacred institution. They dislike Milton as a republican, a rebel, a Cromwellian, an associate of regicides. It is easy to understand that his opposition to Catholicism and Episcopacy must keep him out of favour with many. Others let their disapproval of the virulence and gross language in some of his prose treatises affect their judgment of him as a person in all respects; which perhaps they would not do if they were better acquainted with the controversial manners of

the age. There is some justification for this dis-
taste, and something might be said for the political
and theological die-hards who hate him on grounds
of principles. But a fourth reason for failure to
appreciate Milton's greatness is utterly absurd,
namely the idea that as a Puritan—whatever that
means—he was not and could not be a lover of
beauty. I have occasionally found this notion
strangely intrenched in the minds of college students. Yet it is likely that the entire world in his
time produced no more accomplished man, no
happier amateur of all the fine arts, no mind more
enriched with ancient and modern poetry. His
father was a musician, and so was he. His education in literature began early, was prolonged to an
unusual extent, and was crowned with travel in
Italy, where he was received by scholars and artists as one of themselves.

Another cause of prejudice against Milton as a
person is the incomplete account of his domestic
troubles which has come down to us, from uncom-
prehending, gossipy writers. That his first wife
deserted him and that he depended upon his daughters to read to him and write for him in his years of
blindness, is the sum and substance of it all; and
since this is all, it should excite our sympathy and
make us admire his courage and persistence in the
face of two heartbreaking calamities.

Then there is an unfavourable attitude towards *Paradise Lost* itself, on the part of persons unable or unwilling to dissociate its poetic beauty and its intellectual energy and scope from the specific religious dogmas which underlie it. Because they consider merely fictitious the legend (or legends, for there are two of them tangled up together) of the creation and fall of Adam and Eve in the second and third chapters of Genesis, they are repelled by Milton's acceptance of this material for his poem, forgetting that a similar prejudice would diminish or even destroy their enjoyment of the *Iliad*, the *Odyssey*, the *Æneid*, and indeed almost all epic poems. A more valid reason for dissatisfaction with *Paradise Lost* might well be one's disagreement with Milton's representation of God as a jealous, capricious, and ill-tempered tyrant. But after all, if we substitute the concept "Nature" for the concept "God" and give "Sin" the significance of "Error," much can still be said for the proposition that the wages of sin is death.

A further obstacle to the full enjoyment of *Paradise Lost*, and one big enough to obscure the lovely element of it, which is the subject of this essay, is the not altogether baseless idea that Milton's opinion of women was unjust and unenlightened. Yet, though he does indeed express the theory of woman's inferiority to man which was and generally had been held everywhere throughout historic time, we must remember that in this too he was like most of his predecessors among the world's poets, with the notable exception of Dante; and the evident reluctance and honesty with which he expresses this view, which he felt obliged to entertain because he thought it sanctioned by divine authority, contrasts favourably with the artificial and excessive exaltation of woman which we find in many mediæval romances of chivalry. Still, in spite of these excuses, the most ardent admirer of *Paradise Lost* must admit that it contains several passages in which Milton is betrayed into gross injustice to Eve by a too close adherence to the old theological view of her inferiority and subordination to Adam and her priority in guilt, a view which a celibate clergy for fifteen hundred years had developed out of the pernicious germs in Genesis. Yet in spite of such an inexcusable line as "He for God only, she for God in him," and various pronouncements of her "subjection" to Adam, Milton painted an exquisitely beautiful picture of "the mother of all living."

Let us remember too, as proof of Milton's susceptibility to woman's charms and appreciation of woman's moral virtues, the noble strains of his half-dozen Italian poems and the touching sonnet on his "late espoused saint," of whom he wrote, though blind,

"... Yet to my fancied sight
Love, sweetness, goodness in her person shined
So clear as in no face with more delight."

After the dazzling infinitudes of the first three
books of *Paradise Lost*—the splendours of Heav-
en's court, the terrors of Hell's concave, the high
discourse, horrid conspiracy hatched and dreadful
doom pronounced—books in which the fall of the
angels predominates, we come to sweeter scenes,
more conceivable by a human being "standing on
earth, not rapt above the pole." In the Fourth Book
lines 205 to 288 are given up to a description of
Paradise, all natural and such as eye hath seen and
ear heard, a passage whose beauty and meaning are
both summed up in the lovely verse, "Flowers of all
hue, and without thorn the rose." There, amid every
delight and surrounded by sportive and gentle
beasts, we encounter

"Two of far nobler shape, erect and tall,
Godlike erect, with native honour clad
In naked majesty,"

and the human story opens.

However deeply convinced of the equality of the
sexes, equality consistent with diversity, one cannot
quarrel with the lines,

> "For contemplation he and valour formed,
> For softness she and sweet attractive grace,"

nor can one be other than pleased with Milton's
elaborate explanation that their nudity was a mark
of "simplicity and spotless innocence."

The passage I chose as my text illustrates the
effect of Adam's first sight of Eve. He had thought
himself completely happy, seeing round about him

> "Hill, dale, and shady woods, and sunny plains,
> And liquid lapse of murmuring streams,"

and feeling he was happier than he knew, for he
had no standard, no experience of sorrow or pain
by which to measure his felicity. But when he observed that all other living creatures had compan-
ions, a disquieting fear of future loneliness stole
upon him and he begged his Creator for a companion

> ". . . fit to participate
> All rational delight, wherein the brute
> Cannot be human consort."

His request was granted. The "fair virgin" came,
and "what pleasing seemed" before was doubly,
trebly, pleasing now:

> "Grace was in all her steps, heaven in her eye,
> In every gesture dignity and love."

It was love at first sight, in Adam instantaneous, in
Eve

> "Not obvious, not obtrusive, but retired,
> The more desirable,"

and though she yielded to his will, it was

> ". . . with coy submission, modest pride,
> And sweet, reluctant, amorous delay."

Carefree, happy in the enjoyment of their friendly
world, and with full delight in their own companionship,

> ". . . hand in hand they passed, the loveliest pair
> That ever since in love's embraces met."

Nature rejoiced in their union:

> ". . . all Heaven
> And happy constellations in that hour
> Shed their selectest influence; the Earth
> Gave sign of gratulation, and each hill;
> Joyous the birds; fresh gales and gentle airs
> Whispered it to the woods, and from their wings
> Flung rose, flung odours from the spicy shrub,
> Disporting, till the amorous bird of night

> Sung spousal, and bid haste the Evening-star
> On his hill-top to light the bridal lamp."*

It is a pity that in the rest of Adam's account of this glad hour, theology and the traditional view of "woman's place" come creeping in to sickly o'er the picture "with the pale cast of thought."

Here is an ominous note, predictive of disaster: he loves her indeed, but not as being his equal,

> "For well I understand in the prime end
> Of Nature her the inferior, in the mind
> And inward faculties, which most excel."

To be sure, he observes, somewhat illogically, as one might expect in a lover:

> "Yet when I approach
> Her loveliness, so absolute she seems
> And in herself complete, so well to know
> Her own, that what she wills to do or say
> Seems wisest, virtuousest, discreetest, best."

---

*This passage was paralleled by Wordsworth in his description of a lover's ecstasy, in "Vaudracour and Julia":
> "Earth breathed in one great presence of the spring;
> Life turned the meanest of her implements,
> Before his eyes, to price above all gold;
> The house she dwelt in was a sainted shrine;
> Her chamber-window did surpass in glory
> The portals of the dawn; all Paradise
> Could, by the simple opening of a door,
> Let itself in upon him:—pathways, walks,
> Swarmed with enchantment, till his spirit sank,
> Surcharged, within him, overblest to move
> Beneath a sun that wakes a weary world
> To its dull round of ordinary cares;
> A man too happy for mortality."

In spite of these forebodings, let us deceive ourselves with the hope that calamity is still far off. We
must not think of it as we watch the enamoured pair
sitting in close embrace while about them

> "Sporting the lion romped, and in his paw
> Dandled the kid; bears, tigers, ounces, pards,
> Gambolled before them; the unwieldy elephant,
> To make them mirth, used all his might, and wreathed
> His lithe proboscis,"—

a scene the like of which cannot, in these degenerate
days, be witnessed even at the circus; nor could anyone but Milton have described it in such gorgeous
terms.

As confessed lovers love to do, they tell each
other when and where Love first entered their
hearts, and inquire

> "... *Al tempo de' dolci sospiri,*
> *A che e come concedette Amore*
> *Che conosceste i dubbiosi desiri?*"

So Eve begins with the phrase her daughters have
repeated through the ages, "That day I oft remember, when——"

It augured well for the permanence and success
of their union that, bowing equal hearts, they began
the grateful labour of their days with prayer:

"Hail, universal Lord! Be bounteous still
To give us only good; and, if the night
Have gathered aught of evil, or concealed,
Disperse it, as now light dispels the dark."

Wedded bliss sometimes does not outlast the honey-moon. The test oft comes with the first entertainment of company. We feel sure, however, that Eve will meet it cheerfully when Adam tells her of an expected guest, an Angel, and bids her

"... Go with speed,
And what thy stores contain bring forth, and pour
Abundance fit to honour and receive
Our heavenly stranger."

She complies eagerly and, though untrained and inexperienced, has the natural good sense to know

"What choice to choose for delicacy best,
What order so contrived as not to mix
Tastes, not well joined, inelegant, but bring
Taste after taste upheld with kindliest change."

There are such women still, who need neither cook nor cook-book to meet a sudden emergency with bounty and grace. Eve's housewifely expertness survived her fall and descended here and there to her posterity. This faint approach to levity on my part will perhaps be forgiven if my readers can pardon

Milton's actual plunge into humour in his comment, as the feast is delayed while Adam and the Angel hold discourse a while: "No fear lest dinner cool"; remembering reprimands he had received, and doubtless deserved, for keeping Mrs. Milton waiting while he talked with visitors.

Almost equally amusing, and somewhat puzzling to a modern reader, is Eve's feeling that she should leave the table and let the other two converse alone. This carries us back only a few years, to the time when ladies invariably withdrew when the wine and walnuts appeared. Since there was no polite convention to determine her action, she explained it to herself, lamely I think, by fancying she should enjoy the substance of their talk better at second hand:

> "Yet went she not as not with such discourse
> Delighted, as not capable her ear
> Of what was high. Such pleasure she reserved,
> Adam relating, she sole auditress;
> Her husband the relater she preferred
> Before the Angel, and of him to ask
> Chose rather; he, she knew, would intermix
> Grateful digressions, and salve high dispute
> With conjugal caresses: from his lip
> Not words alone pleased her."

Well for her had it been if such discretion, such dependence on her husband, had continued longer; though I like her better for her girlish self-will. She loved gardening and found it impossible to keep up with the growth of her myrtle and roses while distracted by Adam's looks and smiles; and so she says, "Let us divide our labours;"

> "For, while so near each other thus all day
> Our task we choose, what wonder if so near
> Looks intervene and smiles, or object new
> Casual discourse draw on, which intermits
> Our day's work, brought to little, though begun
> Early, and the hour of supper comes unearned!"

Adam, presentient of danger, objects to her going off alone, and a long argument ensues, in which of course Eve becomes more and more insistent and Adam yields point by point without knowing he is doing so. She had the last word and won by finesse, persisting in her determination though pretending to be submissive; and saying "With thy permission then," off she goes alone to tend her plants,

> ". . . mindless the while
> Herself, though fairest unsupported flower,
> From her best prop so far, and storm so nigh."

Alas! she found in the Serpent, who stole upon her then, a far more subtle debater than her simple-hearted husband, and after an argument not much longer than the previous one, she yielded to the sophistry and flattery of "the spirited sly Snake." If she had stored her mind with knowledge and trained her wits in logic by sharing the table-talk of her husband and the Angel, she would have been better fortified against the Serpent's wiles. We may find in this a point in favour of co-education, but must not forget that the Devil also sometimes goes to college. Having been so dependent on Adam and too modest to join in conversation with the helpful Angel, she fell an easy prey to one who "made intricate seem straight," made her imagine she could "discern things in their causes," made her skeptical of God's word—I refer to that phrase of awful dramatic irony, "Whatever thing Death is,"—made her dizzy with conceit by calling her "Goddess humane." Thus seduced,

> "... Her hand in evil hour
> Forth-reaching to the fruit, she plucked, she eat.
> Earth felt the wound, and Nature from her seat,
> Sighing through all her works, gave signs of woe
> That all was lost."

Here, at the climax of the whole tragedy, we might leave our poor mother to her fate. She had betrayed herself, her husband, and her posterity. Her degeneration followed fast. First came gluttony, "Greedily she gorged without restraint"; then impiety, when she spoke to herself of God as "Our

great Forbidder, safe with all his spies about him";
then cunning and selfish ambition, when she planned
to "keep the odds of knowledge" in her power and
thus render herself "more equal, and perhaps—A
thing not undesirable—sometime Superior" to
Adam; then jealousy, when she fancied God might
destroy her for her crime and Adam take another
wife. This possibility—"a death to think!"—steeled
her heart to make the cruel resolution, "Adam shall
share with me in bliss or woe," to which she adds
hypocritically:

> "So dear I love him that with him all deaths
> I could endure, without him live no life."

To all these vicious thoughts she added idolatry,
doing low reverence to the Tree of the Knowledge
of Good and Evil, and also deceit, when she re-
joined her waiting lover with a lie on her lips:

> "Thee I have missed, and thought it long, deprived
> Thy presence—agony of love till now
> Not felt, nor shall be twice."

The interest of the story now centres about Adam,
who, "soon as he heard

> "The fatal trespass done by Eve, amazed,
> Astonied stood and blank, while horror chill
> Ran through his veins, and all his joints relaxed.
> From his slack hand the garland wreathed for Eve
> Down dropt, and all the faded roses shed."

These last two lines are the most touching and significant in the whole narrative. They depict Adam's single-hearted love and his instant realisation of the disaster, while in the one word "faded," indicating that nature felt the change, Milton's genius, I think, achieves one of its greatest triumphs. What a subject for a painter: Eve with guilt showing through the forced gaiety of her lovely face; Adam dumfounded and horror-stricken; the roses fading and falling between them!

Adam, with a manly loyalty of which his sons may well be proud, does not reproach Eve, but repeats the assurance of his admiration and love of her. He blames not her, but "some accursed fraud of enemy" which has ruined them both; and with courage and devotion equalling any recorded act of chivalry and proving that our first ancestor was a great gentleman, he declares without a moment's hesitation, "with thee Certain my resolution is to die."

This meant of course that he would share her crime and punishment. Weeping for joy that he was "willing to incur Divine displeasure for her sake," she gave him to eat of the forbidden fruit.

> "He scrupled not to eat
> Against his better knowledge, not deceived,
> But fondly overcome with female charm."

We are to infer that he did wrong, and reason as well
as legend tells us so. But the heart cries out on his
behalf.

His degeneration followed immediately, and the
pair of them sank lower and lower till they ended
in a vulgar squabble:

> "Thus they in mutual accusation spent
> The fruitless hours, but neither self-condemning;
> And of their vain contest appeared no end."

Here we might drop the curtain, but to do so
would be unfair to Eve. When Adam, in the Tenth
Book, after the curse has been pronounced upon
them and their seed, looks hopelessly towards the
future and repulses her, calling her "this novelty
on earth, this fair defect of Nature," and insults her,
shouting "Out of my sight, thou serpent!" she offers
to sacrifice herself for him:

> "Both have sinned, but thou
> Against God only; I against God and thee,
> And to the place of judgment will return,
> There with my cries importune Heaven, that all
> The sentence, from thy head removed, may light
> On me, sole cause of all this woe,
> Me, me only, just object of His ire."

This noble offer soothes his angry breast; reconcilia-
tion follows; and equal once more in love and fate,

they implore Divine forgiveness. She bore with
fortitude the sentence to hard labour, not dreaming
it was to be performed elsewhere than in her beloved
Garden, with Adam by her side:

> "Let us forth,
> I never from thy side henceforth to stray,
> Where'er our day's work lies, though now enjoined
> Laborious, till day droop. While here we dwell,
> What can be toilsome in these pleasant walks?
> Here let us live, though in fallen state, content."

Many a man overtaken by illness or loss of property
or position has had his heart thus strengthened by a
faithful wife. But alas! Eve had yet to learn the
full extent of their punishment. They must leave
the Garden, the flowers she has named and "bred up
with tender hand," the nuptial bower she has
adorned. Adam recovers from the blow, and anon
she too is comforted by the promise of "The great
deliverance by her seed to come," and hope springs
up in both of them,

> "... though sad,
> With cause, for evils past, yet much more cheered
> With meditation on the happy end."

When the hour of departure came, she was able
to say to Adam:

"Now lead on;
In me is no delay; with thee to go
Is to stay here; without thee here to stay
Is to go hence unwilling; thou to me
Art all things under Heaven, all places thou,
Who for my wilful crime art banished hence."

More truly lovers now than even in the springtime
of their joy, having shared both happiness and sorrow, they pass out of Paradise and from our sight:

"Some natural tears they dropped, but wiped them soon;
The world was all before them, where to choose
Their place of rest, and Providence their guide.
They, hand in hand, with wandering steps and slow,
Through Eden took their solitary way."

GLORIOUS SIR WALTER

"You know the great Sir Walter died in 1832. Let us all read at least one of his novels this year as a tribute to his memory." Thus I spoke right and left to my friends in January, 1932. At the joyous thought of practicing what I preached, I could see myself as a little boy lying face downward on a boardwalk in the broiling sun with my nose and my entire mind buried in the pages of *Ivanhoe* for six consecutive hours of bliss inexpressible. Then, with less physical exposure but as much mental fever, I had followed the Red Cross under "the burning sun of Syria" as related in *The Talisman*, and pursuing my way northward through *Kenilworth* and *Rob Roy* to the cooler clime of Scotland, had attained hyperborean limits in *The Pirate*. That was long ago, and now some people are telling us that Scott does not appeal to the boys and girls of today. So much the worse for them, say I; and anyhow, Scott wrote for grown men and women, and his best can be fully appreciated only by readers who have lived and observed and felt during at least a score of years, and the longer the better; for as we grow older two subjects interest us more and more, until they absorb nearly all our curiosity and gratify nearly all our intellectual cravings, namely history and human character. This statement, to be sure, does not include those gifted and less common spirits who find their chief satisfaction in science, but I am referring to the generality of mankind. History and human character, then, are what ordinarily attract and edify mature people. Scott's novels are history touched with imagination and expressed through the medium of human character.

As a spokesman once more of the unspecialized reader, I declare that as a rule we learn history through fiction. It is Shakespeare's Cleopatra, Brutus, Antony, and Cæsar, rather than Plutarch's, whom we know or think we know. Who but dear old Dumas really created Richelieu, Mazarin, and de Retz for us? I disdain to come farther down: Shakespeare and Dumas and Sir Walter are enough; and not the least of these as a vivifier of history is the man who has made the English-speaking world as familiar with Scottish lore as we are with the history of any two countries of Continental Europe. Exaggeration? Well, perhaps so, but the subject makes my ink boil. Character-study has been the special province of many novelists since Scott. With some it has been marvellously successful; with others, and especially of late, it has been a doleful obsession, causing pain to the reader and a conceit of wisdom in the author, and occasioning that most maleficent manifestation of pedantry, the development of "schools of thought." Yet Sir Walter, without following the doctrines of any Viennese psychologists, or involving himself in coils like Henry James and Paul Bourget, or sorrowfully probing the extremes of dullness like Galsworthy, created men and women and made them figures in a series of historical pageants. The most important of these figures, considered as works of art, are drawn from the humbler walks of life; but they have imposing significance nevertheless, for they are symbolic reality, they are true and representative.

The man himself is in his works. The Chantrey bust is an image of both. Study it, and what do you see? A character romantic always, heroic when moved to action, humorous, yet in its depths grave and reflective. It is the countenance of a tolerant, open-hearted observer of mankind, one acquainted with the devious ways of human nature and lenient in his judgment of human frailty, while himself wholesome and above all meanness. It is the image of one who was happy and strove to make others happy, a genial, hearty soul in a healthy body. It has the eyes of a poet, a dreamer seeing wondrous visions, though the firm lips show that he possessed plenty of Scotch prudence and self-control. "This man," you will exclaim, "was generous. His virtues did go forth of him. Here are more than enough spirit and strength for a single individual." We can discern also a touch of whimsicality, but nothing perverse, nothing cynical. It is the head of a philosopher of the broad ways of life, no peeping analyst. And what learning dwells behind that noble brow!

His works are in the same proportion, abundant, with enough overflow of power and material to furnish forth a half-dozen quite able and prolific authors. They may be too romantic for readers who wish to be instructed all the time and never diverted; the taste of our age is for realism and propaganda. Perhaps we are justified in hastening through Scott's occasionally prolix descriptions of "sands and shores and desert wildernesses." Still, these lengthy pictorial passages are very well done of their kind—more than that, they are usually faithful reproductions of observed reality; and if we do not relish the kind or are too ignorant to recognise their truth, we can skip a page or two now and then. I have heard one worshipper of Sir Walter say she loves to read his "Introductions" both before and after reading the novels they precede. She is wise, and has her reward in becoming really intimate with the author's own character, which is as grand and beautiful as the best creatures of his imagination.

There are episodes in Scott as heroic as any in Homer. One scene in *Waverley* may serve as an example, out of many that could be chosen. A batch of Scottish prisoners at Carlisle are being tried and condemned to death after the failure of the Jacobite raid in the '45. A Highland chieftain is about to be sentenced when one of his retainers offers the lives of himself and five others of the clan if the judge will release their hereditary leader: " 'If you'll just let me gae down to Glennaquoich, I'll fetch them up to ye mysell, to head or hang, and you may begin wi' me the very first man.' Notwithstanding the solemnity of the occasion, a sort of laugh was heard in the court at the extraordinary nature of the proposal. The judge checked this indecency, and Evan, looking sternly around, when the murmur abated, 'If the Saxon gentlemen are laughing,' he said, 'because a poor man, such as me, thinks my life, or the life of six of my degree, is worth that of Vich Ian Vohr, it's like they may be very right; but if they laugh because they think I would not keep my word and come back to redeem him, I can tell them they ken neither the heart of a Hielandman nor the honour of a gentleman.' There was no further inclination to laugh among the audience, and a dead silence ensued."

This episode has the pathos attendant upon the vain struggle of an ancient but weak civilisation fighting a rearguard action against a newer and more powerful one. Something similar is going on in America today, where the simple and wholesome life of rural communities is being overcome by the ethics of the sidewalks and subways of New York.

Scottish manners among both high and low are portrayed richly in the Waverley novels. Certain aspects of Scottish character, its ironical humour, its pertinacity, its contrasting elements of idealism and hard practicality, are shown in hundreds of places, but perhaps nowhere more brilliantly than in the verbal battles between the antiquary Monkbarns and Sir Arthur Wardour. It might have been expected that a writer so fond of romance, so steeped in local tradition, so fervent in his Scottish nationalism, would have been unfair to England when contrasting the qualities of the two countries; but Sir Walter always deals justly and even handsomely with Scotland's ancient foe, and many of the personages on whom he lavishes his most approving touches are chivalrous, right-minded English gentlemen. He does not take a merely Scottish view of the past, does not grumble, is not vindictive, for he recognises that union and bigness are more to be desired than isolation and independence. In matters of personal conduct, too, his tolerance is admirable. Who does not remember Edie Ochiltree's eloquent and pathetic appeal to the two young hotheads who are about to fight a duel in *The Antiquary?* It contains in a few words enough to have caused any reader to abjure the absurd custom of duelling and forsake the ruinous career of a soldier. A moment later, however, the same voice offers a charitable plea for these misguided men whom the rules of chivalry or the enthusiasm of national warfare have caused to shed the blood of their fellows. The former part runs thus:

> " 'Are ye come here among the peaceful hills, and by the quiet waters, that will last whiles aught earthly shall endure, to destroy each other's lives, that will have but an unco short time, by the course of nature, to make up a long account at the close o't? O sirs! hae ye brothers, sisters, fathers that hae tended ye, and mothers that hae travailed for ye, friends that hae ca'd ye like a piece o' their ain heart? And is this the way ye tak to make them childless and brotherless and friendless? Ohon! it's an ill feight whar he that wins has the warst o't.' "

Edie, I am fain to think, is Scott's best creation and *The Antiquary* his greatest novel. Who can forget the noble old mendicant's first appearance, with his "Prætorian here, Prætorian there, I mind the bigging o't"?

Sir Walter was preserved from religious bigotry in his references to the strife " 'twixt Presbyterie and Prelacie" by the fact that he belonged to a minority sect, being an Episcopalian in a country overwhelmingly Presbyterian; though I am sure his own broadmindedness would have been enough to save him from fanatic zeal. In politics, too, though he was a conservative and stoutly opposed to the Revolutionary movements of his day, he interprets history not merely from the aristocratic standpoint, but had a heart for the common people.

It is the lot of few men, and especially of few men of poetic genius, to lead as happy and full lives as Sir Walter's. He had his griefs and misfortunes, but endured them patiently and bravely, transmuting apparent evil into good. Until obliged by a sense of honour to overwork in order to meet obligations incurred only in part through his own fault, he wrote with ease and joy. Barring only one or two, his novels also radiate happiness. Though they depict with unflinching truth the inevitable woes of life, as, for example, in the heartrending description of the young fisherman's funeral in *The Antiquary*, their general tone is far from tragic. If there be anything to withhold one from reading and rereading the greatest of our recent novelists, Thomas Hardy, it is the knowledge that ineluctable fate sits grimly smiling in the last chapter, and that no good intentions or brave efforts will save her victims from defeat. Scott's books are like glorious summer days: there may be clouds and rain, but sunshine and warmth and colour and the songs of birds prevail. Balzac, powerful and admirable in some aspects, was tainted with a vulgar desire for wealth; many of his novels reflect this failing of the man. Others of them are spoiled by his attempt to load them with what he considered philosophy. Scott's novels are free from sordidness, and such philosophy as pervades them is the logic of common sense, the metaphysics of reverence, the psychology of kindly observation, and the ethics of honour plus charity. They are never dull, whereas Galsworthy, Dreiser, and Bennett seem to have aspired to make their books as drab and flat as possible. Their Muse, whom they have worshipped with many vows and sacrifices, is Dreariness.

Scott's most amazing success, like that of Dumas, is in the conversation of his characters. It is by far the best element of his novels, especially when the scene is Scotland or the speakers, wherever they may be, use the Scots vernacular. The talk of his persons of inferior rank is more vivid and racy than the cultivated discourse of the gentry. He agreed with Wordsworth that in humble and rustic

life "the essential passions of the heart find a better soil in which they can attain their maturity, are
less under restraint, and speak a plainer and more
emphatic language." Acquaintance with the vocabulary of the Scots dialect and also familiarity with
the clear, sweet, flexible tones of speech in Scotland are of course necessary for a full appreciation
of these fine passages. The Scottish voice, in pitch,
tempo, and precision, is more attractive than the
voices one commonly hears in America or even in
England; and to read Sir Walter by ear is a feast
of music. I have said nothing about his marvellous
gift for creating characters. There was no need to
do so. Enthusiasts have placed him beside Shakespeare in this respect. I do not; but if we say he
stands with Dickens and Thackeray and Balzac and
Turgeniev, we shall have said much and told the
truth. Here again, as is the case with his dialogues,
the "simple" excel the "gentle," and his most vital
characters are of low estate and often minor figures
in the stories.

I am constantly looking for really great novels
by living authors, and am almost always disappointed when I follow the recommendations of publishers, critics, or even of my best informed and
most trusted acquaintances. Only three of my recent adventures into contemporary English fiction
have been completely satisfactory, those namely

which led me to Lima with Mr. Thornton Wilder, to Quebec with Miss Willa Cather, and to a London workhouse with Mr. C. E. Lawrence in *The Iron Bell,* the story of Elizabeth, a brave servant girl, who is drawn evidently true to life and with exquisite tenderness, a story as tragic in its evocation of pity and fear and its vision of the ultimate triumph of goodness as a play of Sophocles. Lately, having some leisure and being unwilling to hazard it in experiments, I have been making sure by rereading Scott. Thus far I have gone through *Waverley, Quentin Durward, The Legend of Montrose, Ivanhoe, Guy Mannering,* and *The Antiquary* in the order named. All have given me fresh delight. *The Heart of Midlothian* and *Rob Roy* are to follow as soon as possible. I have been impressed by the evocation of historical characters in *Quentin Durward* and have understood why that small boy, nearly sixty years ago, was so enchanted with *Ivanhoe.* This late reading has given me a higher appreciation of Scott's humour and wisdom than I had before. And I have been especially impressed with the extent and variety of his learning. He was familiar with history, of course, and with Latin literature. He knew Shakespeare by heart and had read widely in the other Elizabethan and post-Elizabethan dramatists. Several branches of recondite lore, including heraldry, genealogy, mediæval military science, folklore, magic, and Scottish local tradition, were his delight.

As I moved eagerly through the pages of *Guy Mannering* I tried to imagine how excited I should feel if some new novel of today should give me equal pleasure and an equal sense of its author's greatness. Wordsworth's sour comment on it, in a letter to R. P. Gillies, just after its publication, in 1815, occurred to me: "The adventures I think not well chosen or invented; and they are still worse put together; and the characters, with the exception of Meg Merrilees, excite little interest." There is more of this harsh criticism, with some truth in it, too, when he condemns Scott's artificial combinations of scenery and episode. One thinks of the many quotations and footnotes by which the great popular novelist went out of his way to familiarise his vast audience with the poems of Wordsworth, which were then comparatively little known. Generosity on the one hand, absolute critical frankness on the other; and happily an unbroken friendship and mutual admiration. It is only fair to Wordsworth to quote here his memorable tribute to Sir Walter—and it is the best ever paid to him—in a letter of October, 1831, after hearing of his apoplectic stroke:

"I trust the world and his friends may be hopeful, with good reason, that the life and faculties of this man—who has during the last six-and-twenty years diffused more innocent pleasure than ever fell to the lot of any human being to do in his own life-time—may be spared."

Not only has no one been the worse for reading Scott; millions have received not merely pleasure but noble impulses, a contribution to their standards of justice, mercy, courage, kindness, and truthfulness. In this respect he almost equals Thackeray, who, in a much narrower field and less copiously, taught the art of being a gentleman (or a lady). No youth or maiden can afford to pass into manhood or womanhood without having read *Henry Esmond*. One forgets that it is fiction. Thackeray is the most complete realist and also a profound believer in the transcendence of eternal goodness. Dickens was, perhaps even more than Scott or Thackeray, a man of sheer genius. There are no more natural and living pages in our literature than some of his. But his qualities are not well balanced and controlled. He sinks frequently below a level which he could easily have maintained had his taste been equal to his power. Thomas Hardy, whom I make bold to name next to these illustrious masters, is the predestinarian of the group. A discouraging sense of impending doom, which pervades nearly all his stories, drives away many readers who would otherwise enjoy his naturalness and his sympathy with all sorts of people. Scott, on the other hand, though open-eyed to sin and grief, and acknowledging that life is an unfathomable mystery, keeps in the sunshine and helps to make the world happier.

No doubt the admirers of Defoe and Fielding, of Jane Austen and Trollope and Hawthorne and Stevenson would wish to bring one or more of them into comparison with Scott. I understand this desire and share this admiration, but still maintain there is a gap between the universal, dynamic, spontaneous creations of Thackeray, Scott, Dickens, and perhaps Hardy, on the one hand, and the more limited achievements of the others. Stevenson is not a whit behind Scott in representing what is romantic and gallant. John Galt reproduced the Scots dialect as well as his great contemporary. But Sir Walter is the "wondrous potentate" of a wider and richer empire than any of these "sceptered kings or laurelled conquerors." His realm includes "whatever clime the sun's bright circle warms," and still, after the lapse of a century,

"the might of the whole world's good wishes with him
  goes."

COLERIDGE'S GREAT AND DEAR SPIRIT

HE WHO would write a general eulogy of Samuel
Taylor Coleridge must be prepared for disenchant-
ment. He will discover a character which proves
weaker the more it is examined and a vast dispro-
portion between promise and achievement. If, however, he suspends his purpose of praising Coleridge
and seeks industriously to measure the quality of
his philosophic thought, the height of his poetic
imagination, the number and variety of his works,
and the extent of his influence, a substantial and
admirable figure will arise, worthy enough of
praise. It is a figure unmistakable and unfading.

Young De Quincey, armed with a letter of introduction to Coleridge, whom he had never seen,
fails to find him at Nether Stowey, and, proceeding
to the neighbouring town of Bridgwater, is driven
by rain to seek shelter under a gateway there. Beside him he perceives a man standing in a reverie,
and recognises Coleridge by "the peculiar appearance of haze or dreaminess" mixed with the light of
his eyes. There was geniality too in that countenance, and an invitation to friendly discourse. The
"Coleridge look" was so marked that it has de-

scended through four generations, as I can myself
testify, for in the tragic winter of 1914-15 my wife
and I, being invited by the late Ernest Hartley
Coleridge to visit him at Aylesbury, found a large
crowd of soldiers and their friends on the station
platform there, but had no doubt which of all those
hundreds of faces belonged to our host, whom we
had never met before. And when we were in his
drawing-room admiring a fine portrait of Samuel
Taylor Coleridge which hung on the wall, a little
girl came in and stood by chance below the picture.
We drew our breath, for the resemblance was as-
tonishing. "I know what you are thinking," said
Mr. Coleridge with a smile: "it's her likeness to
her great-great-grandfather." There must have
been much elemental matter in a man who was so
easily recognisable from the expression of his face
in repose and whose traits were so safely transmitted to his posterity. This unfading quality, this
congruity and continuity of selfhood, needs to be
made evident, for appearances point rather to inconsistency and change.

There is congruity enough, fulfillment and completeness enough in the artistic perfection of what
Coleridge did supremely well, yet popular opinion
robs him of his due praise by regretfully referring
to what he might have accomplished if only——
Fortunately children in school are allowed to enjoy

"The Rime of the Ancient Mariner" without captious comment; it is accepted as a perfect poem. But appreciation is qualified when they read "Christabel" and have to hear the disillusioning remark that "the author could never make himself finish it." When they read "Kubla Khan," with wonder and joy of course, their delight is tainted by the information that it was "an opium dream." Thus enthusiasm is damped, and carping criticism spoils enjoyment of two most glorious poems. Furthermore, unless their teachers happen to be unusually well acquainted with biography, little is done to open to pupils the meaning and consequently the beauty of Coleridge's great conversation poems, such as "This Lime-tree Bower my Prison," "Fears in Solitude," "The Nightingale," "Frost at Midnight," "Dejection," and "To William Wordsworth," and still less to teach them history through his political pieces, such as his "Sonnets on Eminent Characters," "Reflections on having left a Place of Retirement," "The Dungeon," and "France, an Ode." Missing these, they get no knowledge of his humaneness, his public spirit, and think of him perhaps as one of his own "footless birds of paradise," dreaming of unrealities and impossibilities. In Caroline Fox's *Journals and Letters* there is a phrase of her brother Barclay's which describes almost all great poetry—"A plant

that seeks the sun yet grasps the soil." Though the
three poems of Coleridge with which everybody is
familiar are notable exceptions to the second part
of the phrase, since they certainly do not grasp the
soil but hang in mid-air, nearly all his other poetry
is remarkably close to reality and sane experience.
As a record of intellectual history it has, in this
respect, a value that is often lacking in the poetry
of Shelley and Keats and even Byron.

Strangely enough, however, there is little philos-
ophising in Coleridge's poetry, little argument, little effort to persuade. The poet in him was very
distinct from the metaphysician and the propagan-
dist who were so prominent when he talked or wrote
prose. If one knew nothing about him except what
could be gained from his poems and a few notes
necessary to the understanding of them, one would
say: "Here is a very great poet who was also a
very great man, humane, benevolent, religious, of
simple tastes and steady, well-ordered conduct,
probably not extremely learned though widely
read,—a man who led a happy and healthy life,
though in certain passages he gives expression, no
doubt exaggerated, to fears and self-reproach." If
the reader shares the common idea that Coleridge
was a futile, unproductive man of genius, without
balance, inconstant, weak, and unhappy, let him
weigh the adjectives in the preceding sentence in

the light of a full knowledge of what Coleridge
actually wrote and ask himself whether they are
not after all justly applied, except, of course, that
his learning was enormous, his conduct often subject to a weak and diseased will, and his misery
sometimes "foot-thick." These are large exceptions,
to be sure, but there are left the generous desire to
do good, the religious humility, the childlike simplicity, and a godlike power to create. In lines that
express both the wealth of his endowment and a
sense of having squandered much of it, he cries:

> "Imagination; honourable aims;
> Free commune with the choir that cannot die;
> Science and song; delight in little things,
> The buoyant child surviving in the man;
> Fields, forests, ancient mountains, ocean, sky,
> With all their voices—O dare I accuse
> My earthly lot as guilty of my spleen,
> Or call my destiny niggard! O no! no!
> It is her largeness and her overflow,
> Which being incomplete disquieteth me so!"

Among the published poems of Coleridge there
are more fragmentary pieces than can be found in
the "complete works" of perhaps any other author.
This gives an impression of weakness, of inability
to carry out projects and sustain emotional flights.
It is only fair to observe that many of these unfinished poems were not published by Coleridge him-

self but by editors who found them in his notebooks and letters. Very little of Milton's incomplete verse exists—only a few rejected lines in the Trinity College manuscript, and the fragment "On the Passion," to which he appended the remark: "This Subject the Author finding to be above the years he had when he wrote it, and nothing satisfied with what was begun, left it unfinished"; yet it is inconceivable that he could have achieved his perfect artistic mastery without having made many a beginning which he abandoned and composed many hundred lines which he rejected. We should be grateful to Dykes Campbell and E. H. Coleridge for including the fragments in their editions; for many of them are of priceless worth, "gems of purest ray" which otherwise would lie hidden in the "dark unfathomed caves" of oblivion. They are detachable from such contexts as they have, and lose little by the process. I am far from believing that poetic inspiration comes only in flashes and that no passage of real poetry can be longer than fifty or a hundred lines or whatever limit has been set by various persons who have dogmatised on this subject. Merely to *plan* "Paradise Lost" was an act of poetic inspiration, and there is not a line of it that does not proclaim the hand of genius. So too with "The Divine Comedy" and in a less degree "The Prelude." *Per contra* many a poem is the weaker for its author's endeavour to make it systematically complete, for example "The Faerie Queene." Two of Coleridge's most elaborate attempts, "The Destiny of Nations" and "Religious Musings," are failures if completeness be the measure of success, but at least a hundred lines of the former are rich in beauty and significance, and one single line,

"The alien shine of unconcerning stars,"

is sublime and awe-compelling, while in the latter there are "heights most strange, whence Fancy falls, fluttering her idle wing." Yes, Fancy falls, broken-winged and baffled, but from heights seldom attained except by this great poet.

As a reader familiarises himself with the poems—all of them, not merely the famous ones—his opinion of Coleridge's genius rises; he feels grateful for so much gold and cares less and less that it has not all been separated from its original quartz and melted down and fashioned into vessels for ornament and use. Of his contemporaries none except Wordsworth and Keats has given us more of this precious metal; yet men talk of his futility and deplore his failure to round out his undertakings. *Edwin Drood* remains in one's memory, less perishable for being unfinished. *Weir of Hermiston* turns its readers into amateur novelists, each trying to imagine how it ought to be continued. Joseph Conrad would have been well advised to end *Lord Jim* when his unheroic yet very human hero obeys the impulse of self-preservation and deserts his ship. Shakespeare "made a play" but spoiled a great tragedy by adding the last two acts to *Measure for Measure*.

The special qualities of Coleridge's poetry are, it seems to me, a power of creating a sense of reality so vivid that it might be called hallucination, and a power of communicating moral truth. These are the qualities which give Shakespeare his pre-eminence, and none of our other poets possesses so large a share of them as Coleridge. The first is exhibited not only in the three great mystery poems, but in the conversation poems too, where we hear his voice and almost his heartbeats, and see things he sees, and are fain to believe he is talking to us. It gives amazing life-likeness to many passages in the fragmentary pieces, so that here and there suddenly a picture startles us into wondering where we are, as when, in an absolutely detached sentence at the end of "The Destiny of Nations," we read:

> ". . . a landscape rose
> More wild and waste and desolate than where
> The white bear, drifting on a field of ice,
> Howls to her sundered cubs with piteous rage
> And savage agony."

He communicates moral truth not so much in his passages of deliberate reflection as by a general diffusing of his own spirit of loving-kindness, humility, and reverence. In his poems there is none of Byron's cynical hardness, none of Byron's cruel egotism. Though they have not Shelley's childlike and innocent assurance, they possess a compensating maturity of moral judgment. They reveal the man. With the striking and, of course, very important exception of the three mystery poems, they nearly all are his direct utterance, as letters or entries in a diary might be. He is here in his own person, and most attractive, very candid, simple, and pure. The simplicity is what may well astonish us in one with his reputation for endless metaphysical discourse. Poetry was his holy of holies, the citadel of his ambition, not a place for relaxation and secondary thoughts. It was his high calling, and his other occupations—preaching, lecturing, conversing, journalism, politics, theology—were in comparison only means of earning money or exercising his wits or, more frequently, sops to his conscience when it reproached him for inactivity. For poetry he reserved his best moods, his least perturbed moments, his most vivid sensations, his clearest thoughts.

A man who had conceived and completed so magnificent a work as "The Ancient Mariner" at the age of twenty-five must have lain prostrate and awe-struck with the knowledge that upon him too had fallen the inspiration of "that eternal Spirit, who can enrich with all utterance and knowledge, and sends out his seraphim, with the hallowed fire of his altar, to touch and purify the lips of whom he pleases." And if he then determined to add "industrious and select reading, steady observation, insight into all seemly and generous arts and affairs," it was because he, like Milton, "refused not to sustain this expectation" of being an instrument of heavenly music. His friend Wordsworth, by whose side he felt himself "a little man," had hitherto composed nothing so unquestionably great. The stubborn, simple, superstitious, childlike soul of man is its hero, the wide ocean is its scene, its colours are drawn from rainbows, stars, and gleaming water. In the same year he composed "Kubla Khan," that "perfect chrysolite"—perfect even though not "one entire," for blinding beauty makes the eye indifferent to all but what it sees for the moment. In the same year again he composed the First Part of "Christabel," introduction to another magic world. These three pledges of immortality bound Coleridge to poetry as the lady of Heaven's choice for him. Henceforth his other undertakings were ancillary, mere handmaidens to serve the queen. They were not allowed to talk in her pres-

ence. Though her utterances were few, they were
uncontaminated by the various jargons of her court.
She must speak the royal idiom, and only when
she pleased.

The tongue of man wags eternally. Talk aims
not at symmetry, proportion, and a definite ending.
Philosophic speculation always begins anew from
every supposed conclusion. Theology, though
claiming now and then to have enclosed some area
of established truth, always breaks out through an
unstopped loophole and starts off building new
fences. Science glories in the prospect of indefinite
advance and expects to make excursions and even
to run up blind alleys. Art alone, and poetic art
scarcely less than sculpture, aims at unity, simplicity, and a definite finish. *In der Beschränktheit
zeigt sich erst der Meister.* The poet looks to the
end, and for the sake of the end declines invita-
tions to wander from his course. It is only in his
poetry that Coleridge was an artist. Only in his
poetry did he even try to regulate the clamorous
mob of observations, memories, concepts, and purposes that surged in the antechambers of his brain.
By its very nature poetry required him to bar the
door against all unfit, discordant applicants. Hence
the surprisingly small amount of metaphysical
speculation in his verse, the broad, practical, and
by no means controversial teaching in "Religious

Musings," the brevity of the moral epilogue to
"The Ancient Mariner":

> "He prayeth best who loveth best
> All things both great and small."

Hence too the epigrammatic sufficiency of his comments on public men and public affairs, such as
this very early one, composed before he was twenty
years old:

> "Though few like Fox can speak, like Pitt can think,
> Yet all like Fox can game, like Pitt can drink."

To say that he always or even generally achieved
the completeness which poetic art demands would
be untrue. He failed far more often than he succeeded. But he succeeded far more often than is
usually supposed. Poems are not to be valued for
their length, and many short poems of Coleridge
are fully rounded and self-contained. Though we
must regret the unfinished projects, the stark scaf-
foldings of which no use was made, the foundations
on which nothing was built, we may rejoice that
there are few unnecessary prolongations and forced
endings in his poetical works. He restrained his
natural expansiveness, his propensity to go on lux-
uriating from one subject to another without apparent connection. Awed by the clear-eyed goddess,

he put aside his garment and laid his hand upon his mouth.

He had good practice in restraint when translating Schiller's *Piccolomini* and *Wallenstein*. A faithful translator must be servant and master at the same time: he must follow the text without deviation, while creating for the ideas a new expression. Coleridge succeeded admirably in both capacities. His version is sufficiently literal, yet it reads like an original composition, and a very good one too! Sir Walter Scott said Coleridge "made Schiller's *Wallenstein* far finer than he found it," and though the translation had a poor sale and the task of completing it irked Coleridge extremely and was one of his excuses for not finishing "Christabel," there had probably been no previous rendering of a German play better or as good. He had the candour to admit in a note that he had not succeeded with Thekla's song, and it is true, for his

"I've lived and loved, and that was to-day—
Make ready my grave-clothes to-morrow"

is far inferior to Schiller's immortal lines:

*"Ich habe genossen das irdische Glück,
Ich habe gelebt und geliebet."*

Mr. E. V. Lucas, annotating a letter from Charles Lamb to Coleridge dated October 11, 1802, says that Lamb had versified Thekla's song from a prose translation supplied by Coleridge. Between them they might have done better. By way of compensation Coleridge has enriched one of Schiller's finest passages and indeed one of the most beautiful in all German literature, by inserting in Max Piccolomini's speech about the meaning of folklore the glorious lines, not traceable in the original:

> "The intelligible forms of ancient poets,
> The fair humanities of old religion,
> The Power, the Beauty, and the Majesty,
> That had her haunts in dale, or piny mountain,
> Or forests by slow stream, or pebbly spring,
> Or chasms and watery depths; all these have vanished."

His own original dramas, *Remorse* (entitled in its earlier form *Osorio*) and *Zapolya*, are very remarkable compositions. *Remorse,* though it was performed for twenty nights at Drury Lane Theatre, is from the standpoint of reasonableness and natural language one of the most impossible plays in the world. It employs every outrageous license of the most degenerate late Elizabethans, a diction that disregards propriety of time, a prosody exceedingly lax. He said himself: "I tried to imitate his [Shakespeare's] manner in the 'Remorse,'

and when I had done I found I had been tracking
Beaumont and Fletcher and Massinger instead."
The plot is more than improbable and is obscurely
unfolded. If the epithet were not a smooth-rubbed
coin, one might describe *Remorse* as an extreme
example of the "romantic." However, its gloom is
relieved by several purple patches and many a
startlingly vivid line. *Zapolya* is better constructed,
more believable, less crowded with horrors, and
yields more delight. Neither of these plays has the
solid merit of Wordsworth's *The Borderers,* which
is coeval with *Osorio* and to which Coleridge gave
unstinted and generous praise, esteeming it above
his own tragedy. And, by the way, in going through
his works, whether prose or verse, formal publi-
cations or letters, from early years or late, one
finds many tributes to Wordsworth, many acknowl-
edgments of indebtedness to him. This is noble and
lovable and was fully deserved.

To sum up our survey of Coleridge's poetry: it
is more copious and varied than is generally supposed; it is full of rich surprises; it is remarkably
free from the faults and excesses which one might
expect, not abstruse or prolix, but conforming
rather, for the most part, to Milton's prescription,—
"simple, sensuous, and passionate." Notwithstanding his devious chases after various distractions—
psychology, metaphysics, politics, theology—and

his many lapses into mere vagueness, lamentation, and dreams, the pursuit of serious and perfect poetic achievement remained his one great purpose. "I never," he said, "have been able to tame down my mind to think poetry a sport or an occupation for idle hours."

It is interesting to imagine what impression Coleridge's poetry would have made throughout the past century if nothing else had been transmitted from him—none of his other writings and no other knowledge about his life and character. He would have been a singularly clear, monumental figure, which is precisely the contrary of what in fact he is. Fancy the surprise of a person who knew only this figure, on discovering the rest of Coleridge, the vicissitudes of his intellectual and even his physical life, his projects, friendships, family troubles, his conversation, his public lectures, his immense importance as a literary critic, his exertions in philosophy, his theological turnings and burnings, his wanderings in search of health, his tragic struggle with the opium habit, his lack of common sense, his abundance of wisdom, his natural joyousness and humour, his pain, remorse, and despair, with only one hope left—the hope of God's pardon and the compassion of his fellow men!

It was inevitable that he should engage in literary criticism. Creative composition is a most ex-

hausting occupation, but talk is easy, and so, to a
man of his powers, is discursive thought. We find
him, even in his Cambridge days, holding forth to
groups of listeners on the merits of poetry. By
some prophetic instinct it was Wordsworth's poetry.
He had not yet seen the author; the poems were
"An Evening Walk" and "Descriptive Sketches,"
in which only a most penetrating eye could discern
the promise of a revolution in poetic method; yet
Coleridge proclaimed, he first, their originality and
promise. Later, in many a midnight talk and country ramble, he and William and Dorothy hammered
out the new theory of poetry which found expression ultimately in the great Preface to *Lyrical Ballads*. At Racedown, Nether Stowey, and Alfoxden,
in Bristol and London, at Grasmere and Keswick,
the endless talk continued, and like the Wedding
Guest, his listeners could not choose but hear. He
had, to use a lively phrase of his own, "a constitu-
tional communicativeness and utterancy of heart
and soul." Talk was a refuge from the reproving
glances of that goddess Poesy, who demanded more
homage than he had strength to give. But though it
was only secondary as compared with poetry, it
was good talk, the best of its kind, not to be matched
perhaps by any other man alive. Behind it lay
extensive reading in Greek, English, and German
philosophy, acquaintance with classical and pa-

tristic literature, knowledge of the English poets, biographers, and theologians, and as time went on, of German poets and critics recent and contemporary. With French literature he seems not to have been very familiar; and, like the rest of the world outside of Italy in the eighteenth and early nineteenth centuries, he was almost unaware of Dante, whose great name now for all men shines with supreme splendour in the long interval between Virgil and Shakespeare. Robert Southey, Joseph Cottle, and J. P. Estlin, Charles and Mary Lamb, William and Dorothy Wordsworth, Thomas Poole, Hazlitt, De Quincey, and Crabb Robinson were among the first of his hearers and interlocutors; but he poured forth his discourse upon all and sundry who would listen. Between 1806 and 1808, at the Royal Institution, he reduced some of his vast redundancy into lectures on the principles of the Fine Arts and on Shakespeare. Other courses of lectures followed at intervals during the next ten years. They were brilliant improvisations, so charmingly interfused with his genial personality that his audiences endured patiently many rambling flights. Indeed they considered themselves fortunate when he remembered his engagements. Of one series Charles Lamb wrote to a distant friend: "Coleridge has delivered two lectures at the R. I.; two more were attended, but he did not come. It is thought he has

gone sick upon them." This casual behaviour came
to be an old story. His audiences were heroic and
"attended" faithfully, but the lecturer often remained away and often spoke on different subjects
from those promised. The lectures have been preserved chiefly from shorthand notes taken by Crabb
Robinson, John Payne Collier, and others. In spite
of all these titles to oblivion, he ranks as one of
the most subtle investigators of the poetic art
and the most suggestive and illuminating interpreter of Shakespeare. We must not expect to find
a single complete treatise in the mass of his prose,
but of penetrating remarks there are hundreds. It
is our misfortune that he did not take pains to write
out his lectures. Of all his prose works, only
Biographia Literaria has even the appearance—
and it indeed has a false appearance—of being
coherent and finished, though it does contain
chapters of supreme value for literary criticism.
But preparation of another kind was not wanting, and he said truly: "I would not lecture on
any subject for which I had to *acquire* the main
knowledge, even though a month's or three months'
previous time were allowed me, on no subject that
had not employed my thought for a large portion
of my life since earliest manhood, free of all outward and particular purpose." When, by good
luck, he and his audience happened to meet at the

advertised time and place, it must have required
all the magnetism of his inspired countenance and
all their patient respect for his reputed wisdom
to hold them in their seats, for even if he chanced
to speak on the subject announced beforehand, he
roamed over the realm of thought in a concatena-
tion of parentheses. "I envy," he declared, "dear
Southey's power of saying one thing at a time, in
short and close sentences, whereas my thoughts
bustle along like a Surinam toad, with little toads
sprouting out of back, side, and belly, vegetating
while it crawls."

His prose has been pieced together from shorthand reports, passages written from memory by
his hearers, fragments in his own handwriting, con-
tributions to *The Watchman, The Friend,* various
newspapers, letters, and the *Biographia Literaria.*
If the result is exasperating, the fault lies not so
much with his editors as with himself. And what a
lamentable waste of great thoughts and splendid
expressions his neglect entailed! Among those that
have survived—and they are many—the following
may serve as examples: "Verse-makers are not
poets: the poet is one who carries the simplicity of
childhood into the powers of manhood; who, with
a soul unsubdued by habit, unshackled by custom,
contemplates all things with the freshness and the
wonder of a child." Shakespeare, he says, charms

you "to gaze on the movements of Venus and
Adonis as you would on the twinkling dances of
two vernal butterflies."

The most vital parts of *Biographia Literaria* are
the chapters that treat of Wordsworth's poetry and
the Preface to *Lyrical Ballads*. Here we listen to a
dialogue between these two great poets, a friendly
debate, in which Coleridge is trying to modify the
extreme statements of a theory that was almost as
much his as it was Wordsworth's. Though publication of the *Biographia* was delayed till 1817, this
subject had been discussed between them for twenty
years, and we may picture to ourselves the little
"half kitchen, half parlour" in Dove Cottage, William on one side of the hearth contending stub-
bornly for some touch of realism both bold and
bald, "dear Col" on the other, smilingly insinuating
that the world would take it amiss, and Dorothy,
glowing in the firelight with worship for her brother
and all his opinions, yet fascinated by their friend's
eloquence. Wordsworth's great Preface and Chapters 4, 17, 18, 19, and 20 of *Biographia Literaria,*
the one complementing the other, constitute the
most satisfactory treatise on the nature of poetry
ever written, not excepting Aristotle's, which is
more limited in scope.

If the most learned people in Britain and America had combined to lay a wreath on Coleridge's

grave one hundred years ago, the motto on the rib-
bon would probably have been: "He was a defender of the Christian faith." Many of these
learned people had not read his poetry and would
have cared little for his literary criticisms. But a
powerful revival of orthodoxy was then occurring
in the English-speaking world, and Coleridge's
Aids to Reflection, published in 1825, was welcomed as a philosophical support of traditional doctrines, all the more because he had formerly been
a Unitarian preacher and a sympathiser with the
French Revolution. The volume must have been
more bought than read, for there are few antiquarian bookshops today that do not contain one or
more shop-worn copies with the pages still uncut.
To describe it is not an easy task, because, though
by no means void, it is without form, consisting
mainly of about seventy-five so-called aphorisms or
propositions, with comments on the same. I once
heard a friar preaching from an open-air pulpit in
Siena. He stood up at intervals to state in formal
terms the main points of his sermon, and then, seat-
ing himself comfortably and leaning forward, made
the applications. So it is in this odd book, close
dogmatic statements alternating with ungirt, far-
reaching exposition. The scholastic dissertations
of the Middle Ages seem here to be renewed, and
it is easy to fancy ourselves peering through the

dusk of a mediæval lecture-room on a winter afternoon in Padua or Paris. To religious seekers of
our time, concerned less with metaphysical proofs
of Christianity than with questions of its origin on
the one hand and of its application to conduct on
the other, Coleridge's aims and method appear
alike outmoded. His opinions carried weight, however, not only because of his extensive acquaintance
with the writings of English theologians, but because he had considerable knowledge of Kant and
his followers in Germany. One must be prepared
to admit the incredible when dealing with Coleridge: perhaps he had read so much; at least he
had apprehended, for his genius showed itself in
his power of rapid assimilation scarcely less than
in his creativeness, and at all events he was one of
the first to transmit Kant's ideas into English minds.
From Kant apparently he derived his distrust of
the "understanding" or pure logical faculty and
his conviction of the superiority of "reason" or the
moral sense, which distrust and conviction are the
underlying elements of *Aids to Reflection*. His employment of the word "reason" in a sense directly
opposite to its ordinary meaning is a stumbling-
block to readers. We usually think of reason as the
logical faculty, and what he termed "reason"
would better have been called "illumination." No
doubt his great name gave support to orthodoxy

throughout the rest of the nineteenth century, and his fertile mind supplied arguments which were eagerly welcomed and appropriated. Whether they are valid in the face of more recent Biblical criticism is less certain. And did he not, by exalting "reason," under which term he included feeling and instinct as well as moral sense more immediately derived from experience—did he not, by exalting this group of impulses above the logical faculty, which distinguishes men from beasts and wise men from foolish, and is our chief instrument of knowledge, retard the advance of light over darkness? As Alois Brandl suggested in his *Life of Coleridge,* "on this principle of reason he maintained the truth of miracle and prophecy because he believed in Christianity, not the reverse." This is probable enough; much more probable than the opinion of John Sterling, who told Caroline Fox that Coleridge "professed doctrines which he had ceased to believe, in order to avoid the trouble of controversy."

For documentary knowledge of Coleridge's personal history and character there are three principal sources: J. Dykes Campbell's excellent biography, 1893, the two volumes of Letters edited by his grandson, Ernest Hartley Coleridge, in 1895, and the two additional volumes of Letters, edited by Professor Earl Leslie Griggs in 1933. Previous biographers and editors, Cottle, Allsop, Green, Sara Coleridge, Henry Nelson Coleridge, Brandl, were able to produce only imperfect and confused records. By this time there is no excuse for failing to recognise his genius, his charm, his humour, and his goodness. His genius, of course, is universally acknowledged and increasingly appreciated; his charm is reflected in the devotion of his friends; his humour, with all that the word implies—gaiety, perception, freedom from vanity—brightens many a page of the letters; and finally, his long warfare with an inherent weakness and an acquired enemy was not waged in vain, for he obeyed the command, "Be not overcome of evil, but overcome evil with good." The letters would provide a hermit with companionship for many weeks, relieving his loneliness, curing his fanaticism, and restoring him to sympathy with humankind. Though many of them are sad and some are pitiful, laughter prevails over lamentation; and as a storehouse of ideas they are unsurpassed even by Bacon's *Essays*, Ben Jonson's *Discoveries*, or Eckermann's *Conversations with Goethe*.

Imagination smiles at the thought of Samuel Taylor Coleridge migrating to the shores of the Susquehanna. Breadfruit and oranges do not grow on the banks of that river, as the Pantisocrats appeared to believe. Cut off from libraries, book-

shops, and publishers, he would have had to ex-
change the pen for a hoe. Fancy him felling a tree
or ploughing amid stumps and rocks! How he
would have puzzled, yet probably delighted, the
earnest English Quakers, the steady-going German
farmers, and the keen Scotch frontiersmen of Penn-
sylvania! He would have been more completely out
of place in the wilderness than any other of the
hopeful communistic band. If indeed he had fled
from idyllic toil to some near-by college town,
Philadelphia or Carlisle or Princeton, he would
have been the most shining light in America. He
would be mentioned with Thomas Paine, John
Witherspoon, Joseph Priestley, and Thomas Cooper
as a precious gift from Britain to the intellectual
development of the new republic. But he was at
home nowhere, not even in England. From
Brandl's *Life of Coleridge,* which is a jealous
apologia for Germany and greatly exaggerates the
influence upon him of Kant and Schlegel, one might
suppose him a mislaid German. He seems to have
thought of himself at times as a neo-Platonic Alex-
andrian born out of due time. Charles Lamb, in
calling him "an archangel a little damaged," gave
him an origin and habitat not of this world. These
speculations about him, this impression of his
uniqueness, this sense of something in him incongruous with his setting in time and place, do not

arise from the perusal of his poetry but from his
letters and the records of his conversation and from
descriptions by persons who saw and heard him.
A typical instance is the effect produced on a certain Captain Ingram, as reported by Caroline Fox.
This not particularly intellectual gentleman frequently met Coleridge at the Gillmans', "and
though as a rule not appreciating such things, spoke
with rapture of the evenings with him, when he
would walk up and down in the glories of a swelling monologue, the whole room hushed to deepest
silence, that not one note might be lost as they lis-
tened to the strains of the inspired poet." The
names and honour of Doctor and Mrs. Gillman
should never be allowed to fade from grateful memory. They took the broken, discouraged victim of
weakness and disease into their home and kept him
there for the last eighteen years of his life, with
what sacrifice of their own tranquillity may be
imagined.

There were at that time in London two eminent
chairs of philosophy, or rather of the *omne scibile*.
The professor in Chelsea described his rival of
Highgate in several deeply etched pen-pictures,
mordant and painful. It is no less just than deco-
rous to cover the cruelest and repeat the most appreciative of Carlyle's lines: "Coleridge sat on the
brow of Highgate Hill in those years, looking down

on London and its smoke-tumult, like a sage escaped from the inanity of life's battle, attracting towards him the thoughts of innumerable brave souls engaged there." And again he mentions his "strange, brown, timid, yet earnest-looking eyes, a high tapering brow, and a great bush of grey hair," and reports, "He is a kind, good soul, full of religion and affection, and poetry, and animal magnetism. His cardinal sin is that he wants *will*. He has no resolution. He shrinks from pain or labour in any of its shapes." All the more wonder then, it seems to me, that in a life not long nor healthy nor spent in steady industry, this man should have made himself justly famous as a disseminator of philosophic ideas, a literary critic eminent for originality and suggestiveness, and a great English poet. Of his bare human worth apart from the glamour of his learning and genius, it is enough or almost enough to say that William Wordsworth was his friend through many trials and Dorothy Wordsworth loved him tenderly; that practical Thomas Poole trusted him and Charles Lamb was proud of having known him since boyhood; that the Gillmans stood by him to the end; and that his children revered his memory.

There are several scenes connected with Coleridge's early life which I prefer even to Hazlitt's famous description, for they testify to his charm by showing the effect he produced upon those who knew him best. At Grasmere, one day in 1800, Dorothy Wordsworth wrote in her journal: "At 11 o'clock Coleridge came, when I was walking in the still clear moonshine in the garden. He came over Helvellyn. Wm. was gone to bed, and John also, worn out with his ride round Coniston. We sate and chatted till half-past three . . . Coleridge reading a part of 'Christabel.'" On the sixth of February, 1802, she wrote: "Two very affecting letters from Coleridge; . . . I was stopped in my writing and made ill by the letters." A few days later she and William walked on a cold, wet evening to Rydal for letters. They met the postman, who gave them two: "We broke the seal of Coleridge's letter, and I had light enough just to see that he was not ill. I put it in my pocket. At the top of the White Moss I took it to my bosom,—a safer place for it." Against the fact that he was often a sore trial to all his friends and especially to these two who loved him most, may fairly be set their joy in his companionship and their profit from his fertile mind. They knew and the world now knows that he accused himself too severely when, with a heart forlorn, he voiced his

"Sense of past Youth, and Manhood come in vain,
And Genius given, and Knowledge won in vain."

It is unjust and cruel to measure men and women by what they might have done. If they strove to do more, let us recognise the effort and not talk about failure. If they did much, let us be thankful therefor.

When Coleridge died, Charles Lamb, so soon to follow, expressed his own and also the general feeling of loss: "His great and dear spirit haunts me. Never saw I his likeness, nor probably the world can see again"; and he went about repeating mournfully, "Coleridge is dead."

THE MAGNANIMITY OF CHARLES LAMB

"Out of the strong came forth sweetness."

IF THE writers of some recent books and articles on Charles Lamb had pondered Samson's riddle they might have spared themselves much vain and tiresome psychological speculation. They seem to have been puzzled by the fact that a man whose life was clouded by a dire disaster and cramped by narrow circumstances could retain a healthy and joyous disposition. They have sought a recondite explanation for the natural play of a rich and happy spirit and imagined that he deliberately had recourse to humour as an "escape mechanism,"—to use one of their horrid terms. Lamb's moral and intellectual strength was not appreciated in his own time, nor has it received full acknowledgment during the hundred and two years since his death. His readers often fail to perceive that the delightfulness of his writings is the flowering of strength.

I would fain write of Charles Lamb's magnanimity. It has two aspects: great-heartedness and great-mindedness. His great-heartedness was primarily a gift of nature, but in large measure also the result of an unusual and awful experience of sorrow, universalised by contact with people of many sorts, wise and foolish, educated and unlettered, rich and poor, independent and conventional. His great-mindedness, the intellectual strength which enabled him to pierce through literary conventions of a century and a half and appreciate the quality of our older poetry, was a form of courage and originality: he wandered along unfrequented paths, freely gazing, boldly admiring.

When his sister Mary killed their mother in a fit of insanity, he not only devoted himself to taking care of her, but made the sacrifice without question or complaint. This was great-hearted indeed. He wrote to Coleridge, in 1798, that he had "well-nigh quarrelled" with Charles Lloyd because "he was drawing me *from* the consideration of my poor dear Mary's situation rather than assisting me to gain a proper view of it with religious considerations. I wanted to be left to the tendency of my own mind, in a solitary state, which, in times past, I knew had led to quietness and a patient bearing of the yoke." The affliction was, in the course of time, softened and even transformed into a blessing by the mutual love and helpfulness that enlarged both Mary's life and his. He was constant in his care of her during her repeated attacks. The strain of expecting and anticipating them must have been

almost harder to bear than the downright misery of
these periods. In the intervals of health, which,
largely through his ministrations, were many and
long, he consecrated himself to making her happy;
and it seems likely that her intellectual and social
joys at these times almost compensated for what
she suffered when her bright spirit was clouded.
He brought interesting people to see her. He was
her faithful companion, himself the most interesting of all her acquaintance. He encouraged her to
write, and the knowledge that she shares his page
in the history of our literature would give him
deeper satisfaction than any other message we could
send him now.

With equal fortitude he accepted the privations
imposed by lack of money. For him there could be
no university education. He was, as he pathetically
said, "defrauded in his young years of the sweet
food of academic institution." Though he built a
fairly handsome superstructure on the sound classical foundation he had gained at school, it was done
by private reading. His essays and letters, which
delight and feed our minds, were composed in the
evening, after the daily drudgery of keeping accounts for the East India Company, whose affairs
were of no interest to him. He seldom had means
or opportunity for travel. A short vacation now
and then, a hurried visit to Nether Stowey in the

west or Grasmere in the north, was all he could afford. With a brave grimace he pretends not to care much for mountains, lakes, and country life; the streets of London, he protests, are more to his taste than the flowery lanes of Arcady; but there is more bravery than truth in these assertions, and they hide a face of pain.

In his day even more than in ours it was a mark of magnanimity when an educated man, of high estate intellectually, was free from excessive class feeling, able to hold up his head in the presence of wealthy or titled people, and also able and willing to meet the poor, the commonplace, and even the really low, on a basis of sympathetic understanding. How unhappy we make ourselves by feeling different from the fellow beings with whom we come in contact, embarrassed by unconscious jealousy and rendered unnatural and inhuman by all-too-conscious pride! Lamb's great heart never had to suffer these ridiculous pangs. His self-respect preserved him from snobbishness; his respect for his fellow men forbade him to stand aloof in hard disdain. For more than a century, patronage had been a chief support of English men of letters. With Lamb we come into the era of paid journalism; and even if his pay was pitifully small, it was enough, with what he earned at the East India House and the little that Mary received for her

stories, to keep both of them alive. Though independent of patronage, they were very dependent on
social intercourse. Some of the most fertile-minded
persons in England—Coleridge, William and Dorothy Wordsworth, Hazlitt, Godwin, Mary Woll-
stonecraft—frequented their lodgings; they knew
several actors and actresses of contemporary re-
nown; the theatre was their delight; the clerks bend-
ing over their ledgers at Charles's elbow; the mar-
ket-women in Covent Garden; shopkeepers with
their curious wares; the vast tide of humanity that
ebbed and flowed through Fleet Street and the
Strand; of all these none was so dull, so ignorant,
so degraded as to escape his appreciative eye or
fail to touch his sympathetic heart. "To the strict
labours of the merchant's desk By duty chained,"
he neither despised the means by which "he humbly
earned his bread" nor failed to do harder and
higher work "when the precious hours of leisure
came."

Lamb should be the business man's saint, for he
kept his ledgers faithfully—"my works," he called
them—and yet in his own free time read more and
to better purpose than many a cloistered scholar,
and developed a rare and lovely literary style. He
should be held in peculiar honour by the millions
in vast cities pent, for he found poetry where no
flowers bloomed and no bird sang. Women should

adore him, not only for his lifelong heroic devotion
to Mary, but because he treated all women with
respect, not reserving his politeness for youth,
beauty, or position. His essay on "Modern Gallantry," with its account of "that pattern of consistent gallantry, Joseph Paice of Bread-street-hill,
merchant," ought to be read by every lad. It offers
a surprisingly simple, yet effective solution of "the
problem of sex." Lamb's nature was large enough
to take in all mankind, and if he excluded the
Scotch, it must have been because he did not know
them, for there was in him much of the Caledonian
ease of intercourse and liveliness of imagination.
He honoured man as man and was a noble by virtue
of being a practitioner of equality.

His great-mindedness, or intellectual superiority,
was due to his independence. The privations and
sorrows of his early life threw him back upon himself and made him his own teacher, his own critic.
For a century and a half the plays of Shakespeare's
contemporaries and immediate successors, with a
few exceptions, had been little read and less appreciated. Lamb, picking up old copies in bookshops and finding them full of glorious passages,
enjoyed them without deference to traditional opinion and made their beauties known to the world
once more. To him, with Coleridge, belongs the
credit for a revival of interest in the rich field of

early seventeenth-century drama. At the same time
he heartily enjoyed the Restoration drama, so much
less poetical, so limited in social scope, so unreal
morally; and no more skillful defense of it could be
made than he set up in his essay "On the Artificial
Comedy of the Last Century"—a defense, however,
which is at the same time a condemnation, as if a
judge should say to an ingenious rogue, "Your im-
pudence fascinates me." Of even greater service
was Lamb's independent taste when he discovered
the charm and manifold richness of English lyric
poetry in the time of Milton. No age in any country has produced more abundant, more varied,
more musical poetry than this; yet the example of
France, the authority of Dryden, and the exclu-
siveness of eighteenth-century taste had cast it almost into oblivion. Lamb followed his whim, un-
concerned about fashion. Largely because of his
intellectual independence, Herrick, and Herbert
and Donne, Vaughan and Crashaw, Marvell and
Wither, Carew and Suckling have come into the
sunshine once more. A notable thing about them is
that they are extremely individual. They never
formed a "school," and absolutely refuse to be
classified. This may be one reason why they at-
tracted Lamb, who was happily incapable of apply-
ing scientific methods to literature. He was the
least pedantic of scholars. He loved to browse in

the *Anatomy of Melancholy,* but did not much in-
vestigate Burton's "sources." His favourite prose
author, and the one upon whose style he modelled
his own in so far as it is at all derivative, was Sir
Thomas Browne; but he was satisfied to enjoy him
without analytical "research." Though his reading
in the ancient classics was fairly broad, it did not
over-shadow the tender green of his English garden.
He read them in the pleasant and extremely profitable way they were read by Spenser, Sidney, Marlowe, and many other Renaissance men; that is to
say, with more regard to substance than to syntax.
Like the Elizabethans, he assimilated knowledge
with reckless appetite, transforming it to suit his
need.

Like many other English writers of his generation, he seems hardly aware that *The Divine
Comedy* existed or that a great new literature was
being created in Germany. To French literature
he seldom refers. These are drawbacks perhaps,
and yet if, through expanding into foreign fields, he
had been able to devote fewer of his midnight hours
to Beaumont and Fletcher and Dekker and to Fuller
and Walton, and above all to Milton, whether in
prose or verse, we should have been the losers.

He preserved a manly freedom from literary
cant. His canons of criticism were his own. One
cannot imagine him using the dialect of a clique or

striving to suit the sickly taste of a coffee-house coterie.

He was free also from political prejudice, not bitter like Hazlitt, worried like Wordsworth, over-whelmed like Southey, dogmatic like Godwin. His democratic instincts and human sympathies never made him desperate. Of course, seeing day by day the suffering of the poor, how they were oppressed by many unjust laws and customs, how cramped and sordid were their lives, he could be no Tory. His generation was probably less cruel than its predecessor; yet it tolerated many shameful prac-tices; and here and there in the *Essays of Elia* we catch a cry of pain. Lamb remembered after the lapse of thirty-five years the tortures inflicted on the boys of his old school. He sang the praise of chimney sweepers, but not without a shudder for the hideous dangers to which they were subjected. The poor, then as now, were wonderfully patient. Whether this trait of patience under oppression be admirable or not, he shared it. Let us hope that all men, a hundred years hence, will look back upon present methods of coal-mining with the same amazement and horror with which we regard the brutalities of Lamb's day.

From religious bondage also he was free. He had religion. It was the power that upheld him in dis-tress. It gave him insight, understanding, the will to help. It kept him happy at times when most men would have mourned or moped. He was reverent, humble, charitable, a true Christian. Little doctrinal baggage did he carry, however, and his faith was the evidence of things seen, rather than of things not seen. The Bible enriched not only his vocabulary but his thought; yet it was not for him, as for so many of his contemporaries, an unerring authority. He was too widely read for that. He was more than tolerant of theologians, understanding, for example, Coleridge's craving for systematic ordering of belief. Having grown up within sound of many church bells and peered through many open church doors and lingered often in the radiant gloom of Westminster's fane or Paul's, he comprehended, though he did not share, the ritualist's æsthetic mood. He was inwardly free, and outwardly un-attached to any creed or sect. He held the belief of Unitarians and emulated the conduct of Quak-ers. There was nothing morbid in his religion. It was a source of peace and a spur to benevolence, not an instrument of self-torture. Apparently he was untroubled by the foul and blasphemous super-stition of eternal punishment, which flourished still in his day and survives here and there in ours. Cruelty was what he most hated, and cruelty on the part of an omnipotent God was to him unthinkable. By quietly assuming the goodness of God, Lamb helped to relieve men's minds from such foul imagining.

Mr. E. V. Lucas, to whom as editor and critic of Lamb the world is most indebted, speaks of him and Coleridge as "shrewd and humorous intelligences." The phrase is apt and should be a warning to those who pick out a lively taunt or sharp retort in the letters of these dear friends and write sad pages about a supposed quarrel between them. They were no doubt at times a little "shrewd" in the old sense of "peppery," but their humour carried them easily over the awkward bumps of debate. It would be a pretty state of affairs if all acerbity between old and tried acquaintances should be magnified into "quarrels." Friendship gives warrant for frankness. Humour excuses exaggeration. Intelligence makes allowance for temper. Imaginative people sometimes enjoy indulging in what onlookers mistake for a fight. Even Mr. Lucas, I am tempted to think, sees too much in Coleridge's remark: "Poor Lamb, if he wants any *knowledge* he may apply to me," and the sarcastic theses with which Lamb retorted. I should not have thought it possible to suppose so intelligent and humourous a man as Coleridge could have made that remark as anything more serious than a somewhat pungent jest. Otherwise it would have been perfectly asinine. And Lamb's response is elaborately playful, though his feelings may have been a little ruffled. What he really thought is expressed in the words he wrote in an album a short time after Coleridge's death: "His great and dear spirit haunts me. . . . He was my fifty years old friend without a dissension."

It is a pity Wordsworth could not have seen more of Lamb, for intercourse with this "shrewd and humorous intelligence" might have made him less dogmatic as he grew old. Their meetings were infrequent, and Lamb, younger by five years, was respectful rather than cordial. He appreciated Wordsworth's genius, and, like Sir Walter Scott, took many occasions to quote his poetry. He saw more of Godwin and Hazlitt. The former was beyond the reach of his humour, the latter below the realm of his goodness.

He was fond of life and life's image, the stage. He made no pretense of wooing death. "I am in love," he says, "with this green earth; the face of town and country; the unspeakable rural solitudes, and the sweet security of streets. I would set up my tabernacle here." How healthy, sane, and honest a declaration! And how different from the sentimental language of many poets in his day, and in ours too! In a letter to his young friend, Robert Lloyd, who was nursing a romantic melancholy, he wrote: "You say that 'this world to you seems drained of all its sweets!' At first I had hoped you only meant to insinuate the high price of Sugar! but I am afraid you meant more. O Robert, I don't know what you call sweet. Honey and the honey-comb, roses and violets, are yet in the earth. The sun and moon yet reign in Heaven, and the lesser lights keep up their pretty twinklings. Meats and drinks, sweet sights and sweet smells, a country walk, spring and autumn, follies and repentance, quarrels and reconcilements, have all a sweetness by turns. Good humour and good nature, friends at home that love you, and friends abroad that miss you, you possess all these things, and more innumerable, and these are all sweet things."

He took a boyish pleasure in food and drink. He loved company and talk, with puns and quips and gossip. It was not his custom, we may be sure, nor that of Mary and their intimates, to sit in Carthusian silence "enjoying each other's want of conversation." Even the small details of domestic life, the placing of a picture or a piece of furniture, the purchase of a leg of mutton, interested him. He was genially domestic and loved his own fireside. He and Mary could not afford long journeys, but they travelled much in the realms of gold. They read incessantly, not merely in the thickly settled and well-known continents, but in the Africas and South Seas of the world of books.

It is consoling to know that though Mary was subject to returns of her malady, she was eminently sane in the intervals of health; and though Charles was never free from anxiety, his outward cheerfulness no doubt sprang from natural serenity of soul. A just, reasonable, and humorous disposition was their notable and saving quality. In Charles's case this is universally recognised; and anyone who has read Mary's letters to Sarah Stoddart must be struck with the soundness of her judgment and the resourcefulness of her tact. Miss Stoddart, who was so lucky as to be sought in marriage by many lovers, appealed to Mary Lamb for advice as each new suitor proposed to her. She was unlucky enough in the end, for she chose William Hazlitt, who made her wretched. But this was not Mary's fault; and the joy of receiving her serio-comic, kind, wise, and witty letters must have been some compensation to Sarah for accepting a bad husband.

It would be impossible to praise too highly Lamb's behaviour as a brother. He restored to a useful and happy life one who without his energetic intervention would have been doomed to a miserable existence. He stood ready to sacrifice for her all his literary prospects, but was able in the end to share them with her by making her the partner of his labours. What has been less generally observed is that his friendly help had a much wider range. To his distant correspondent, Manning, in China, it must have been like visits home to receive the long delightful letters which Lamb wrote to him with great regularity. Coleridge in his moods of desperate discouragement could always find comfort in the thought that his old friend and schoolmate loved him. To those restless and aspiring youths, Charles and Robert Lloyd, his counsel was of inestimable worth. Charles, the elder brother, had to be dealt with carefully, for he thought himself a poet, a man of genius, slighted by his friends. Lamb tolerated his peculiarities and served as a buffer between him and the world he understood so little. Robert was more amiable, and Lamb could both reprove and praise him. He helped the lad through a period of morbid craving for appreciation, telling him, "Our duties are to do good, expecting nothing again; to bear with contrary dispositions; to be candid and forgiving; not to crave and long after a communication of sentiment and feeling." Lamb's blundering old friend George Dyer was perhaps the man he loved best and made most fun of,—Dyer, the plodding hanger-on of Phœbus's car, destitute of humour, uselessly learned, but of sound principles and unwavering fidelity.

Now, "to commit him with his peers," the great

essayists of the world: I find Lamb more winsome,
more lovable than Montaigue, though narrower in
scope and not so experienced in big affairs; of less
strong a wing, though with a sweeter note, than
Bacon; more of a living presence than Addison or
Steele; less austerely compulsive, though in some
unassuming way hardly less ethical, than Emerson.
He belongs to the family of Sir Thomas Browne.
The seventeenth-century physician was amazed and
perplexed by the complicated wonders of the universe and of his own mind, and would probably
not have approved of Lamb's easy shutting of his
eyes to certain mysteries. Browne turned the problems over and over, making guesses that were not
devoid of insight and humour; Lamb either solved
them by moral rule of thumb or gave them up, smiling at his limitations. Nevertheless, Browne is
Lamb's spiritual father and also the begetter of his
literary style. In a later generation the same lively
blood was to fill the veins of Robert Louis Stevenson, and the same style, with modifications of
course, was to reappear in his essays.

There is scarce a page of Lamb's essays or of his
letters which could be mistaken for the writing of
anyone else. His fingerprints are recorded on
Olympus, and no counterfeits pass current. The
style is his own, though its elements can be traced—
and it is a pleasure to look for them—in those old

folios he loved, books written by strong-minded, unregimented individuals who lived in Milton's day and shared his independence. His phrases "smack of the rough magnanimity of the old English vein," of which, however, there are many varieties. We may not speak of *the* style of Ben Jonson, Bacon, Hooker, Bunyan, Jeremy Taylor, Burton, Walton, Milton, Browne, and the several parts of the English Bible, meaning a style common to them all or to any number of them. No other literature and no other period of our own is so rich in widely divergent yet strongly marked *styles*. The geniality and ease of Lamb's writing are due no doubt to his practice as listener and talker. He takes us into his confidence. We feel his presence and know he is aware of ours and politely considerate of our ignorance and prejudices. However, when all is said about his reading and conversation, there remains of course an ultimate something in his style which defies analysis and is simply Lamb himself.

The *Essays of Elia* are not a whit more characteristic than Lamb's letters. The great edition of *The Letters of Charles and Mary Lamb* which we owe to Mr. Lucas is what I should recommend to relieve the tedium of a two-years voyage in a sailing-vessel or alleviate the mournfulness of solitary confinement or populate a desert island for some poor castaway. They reproduce life. They create in the reader vivid images of the persons to whom they were addressed or whom they mention. We are made to share the interests and listen to the talk of a mixed group and hear their opinions of one another. It is all very dramatic, with comedy prevailing over tragedy, for the stage-manager is Humour itself. Our lonely anchorite, at sea, in prison, or enisled, would here find fun as well as wisdom, which he would not do were he limited to Goethe's *Conversations,* with their solemn profundities. He would be allowed to entertain some of that wholesome dubiety which comes with free give and take and is absent from Doctor Johnson's dogmatic monologues. Even the two great collections of Coleridge's letters, the one edited by Ernest Hartley Coleridge, the other by Mr. Earl Leslie Griggs, would be less agreeable society, for a solitary soul would sicken with Coleridge's descriptions of his own woes. Of course there would be one serious limitation, for as Lamb said himself, in everything that relates to science he was "a whole Encyclopædia behind the rest of the world." And I confess that as I write these words and hear the death-dealing motor-cars raging in the street and the death-courting airplanes roaring in the sky, and the telephone, a useful creature, interrupting my communion with the placid soul of Charles Lamb, my lack of knowledge and even of curiosity about the structure of these machines appears to me almost justifiable. Our sailor, exile, or prisoner could very well get along without newspapers too, since, as Lamb says truly, "No one ever lays one down without a feeling of disappointment." A railway journey over a too familiar route is, like solitary confinement, endured piecemeal; and I know a lady who has, a hundred times, brightened such dull trips by reading *Elia* in the train.

If I have mentioned chiefly Lamb's essays and letters, it is because it is in these that he is supreme; but it would be a strange omission not to add that in a few lines of verse rarely equalled for tenderness and pathos he placed himself among the English poets.

When the clatter and rush of life's journey, often disconcerting, often unlovely, make us yearn for quieter times, we have only to open the fair pages of Charles Lamb, like the lady in the train, and lo! the speed abates, green fields appear, and quaint old city streets give us welcome, while all the noise is turned to lovely melody.

WORDSWORTH'S POETICAL TECHNIQUE

No INTELLIGENT and well-informed reader can fail to perceive the underlying purposes and general meanings of Milton, Dryden, Pope, Shelley, Byron, Tennyson, Arnold, or Hardy. Their views of life are unmistakably reflected in their poetry. When these views change, the conversion finds immediate acknowledgment and record. Milton, for example, living through several periods of abrupt and dangerous transition in politics and religion, when persecution was ever imminent, risked his liberty and perhaps his life by being thus frank; yet his theological evolution, at least, is distinctly traceable in his writings, and some knowledge of it helps us to comprehend and enjoy them. There can be no dispute about where Dante stands with reference to Christian doctrine or Florentine politics or the relation between the Papacy and the Empire. The Greek dramatists, no less than Ibsen and Shaw, reveal without equivocation their political, social, and theological ideals. If the Elizabethan dramatists were less inclined to voice their personal opinions on subjects of public controversy, it is because the policy of the government was to let sleeping dogs lie, and also because theatrical success depended on pleasing large, mixed audiences in whom the flames of dangerous controversy might easily have been kindled.

If Wordsworth has been misunderstood—and he has been more frequently and for a longer time misunderstood than any of the writers I have mentioned—it is not because he avoided making his theoretical positions evident. His first great change, from acquiescence in the poetic fashion no less than the philosophic conventions of the eighteenth century, to the Revolutionary doctrine and its application in literature, should have been plain enough without the direct testimony of his Preface to *Lyrical Ballads,* in 1800. On the other hand, before the researches of Professor Arthur Beatty and other scholars, few readers could be expected to see that such poems as "We Are Seven" and "Anecdote for Fathers" were composed specifically to illustrate David Hartley's theory of the association of ideas. The character, extent, direction, and chronology of his second great change, which determined the subjects and tone of most of his later poetry, were strangely overlooked for many years, though they are sufficiently indicated by diction, syntax, and other technical features. Even Arnold, for all his profound intuition of the beauty of Wordsworth's poetry and his noble desire to extend Wordsworth's fame, raised a barrier against complete appreciation by declaring that "we cannot do him justice until we dismiss his formal philosophy." To this I would reply that no one ever did him justice who failed to perceive what his formal philosophy was in his early manhood and how it changed in the course of his long life. Thus, if, without offending the shade of Arnold, whom I gratefully admire, I may turn against him one of his own piercing phrases, it was, even after the publication of his memorable essay, "still quite permissible to speak of Wordsworth's poetry, not only with ignorance, but with impertinence." He was endeavouring, very commendably, and as it proved, successfully, to combat a tendency to regard Wordsworth too much as a political and religious oracle and too little as an artist. Had he not been possessed with this purpose, it must have been evident to him as a fellow craftsman that Wordsworth's poetical technique was to a noticeable extent affected by his philosophy, that is, by the three stages of his psychological studies and of his convictions about the mutual relations of God, Man, and Nature. In each of these periods the material forms—types, metres, vocabulary— of his poetry were determined by the ideas he desired to promulgate and the audience he desired to address.

Let us merely glance at one or two phases of
this alliance between purpose and technique. When
he was very young and not yet quite freed by the
Revolutionary doctrine of human equality from
the traditional feeling that a poet should address
a sophisticated class of readers, he could write in
Descriptive Sketches, composed between 1790 and
1792, such "gaudyverse" as the following absurd
description of an Alpine hunter's predicament on
a steep icy slope (lines 395-398 of the edition of
1793):

> "To wet the peak's impracticable sides
> He opens of his feet the sanguine tides,
> Weak and more weak the issuing current eyes
> Lapped by the panting tongue of thirsty skies."

In plain terms, the unfortunate man cuts a vein in
his foot in order to make sticky spots on which to
tread, but the blood evaporates and he grows faint!
  Fettered by the limitations of the rhymed couplet, constrained to end every line with an emphatic
word, eager to produce a sensation, and not yet
animated by a conviction of the right of all men,
even "uncultivated" men, to enjoy art, the youth
who was to become a great poet, renowned for the
naturalness of his language, penned those ridiculous lines. With their obscurity, pedantry, and pre-
tentiousness compare the plain, honest quality of

these, from "The Old Cumberland Beggar," written in 1797, after his conversion to the Revolutionary philosophy:

> "His age has no companion. On the ground
> His eyes are turned, and as he moves along,
> *They* move along the ground; and evermore,
> Instead of common and habitual sight
> Of fields with rural works, of hill and dale,
> And the blue sky, one little space of earth
> Is all his prospect."

For the highly artificial heroic couplet he has sub-
stituted the more natural unrhymed iambic pentam-
eter; there are no elaborate and unusual expressions; there is only one, very slight, inversion; the
word-order is precisely that of prose; the language
fits the sense, and the sense is within the reach of
any normal grown person's understanding. It is
apparent that between the writer's twenty-first year
and his twenty-eighth a thorough change in his
outlook on life has occurred.

Throughout the next decade, between 1797 and
1807, certain stylistic phenomena begin to appear,
which, of themselves, even without biographical
support, betoken an alteration in the author's point
of view. The sonnet is a highly developed form of
art and lends itself more readily to condensed and
symbolic diction than to an easy flow of language

adapted to the understanding of people not spe-
cially educated; and Wordsworth chose the sonnet as the vehicle of his patriotic emotion, which
he had held in check until his visit to Calais in
1802. From that date his Revolutionary fervour
diminished and was replaced, by slow degrees, with
distrust for advanced measures of social reform, so
that he became a type of extreme political conservative.

Another gradual change in style accompanied
and reveals his return to religious orthodoxy. In
so far as this conversion resulted from the exercise
of his reason and from sound spiritual experience,
he cannot justly be blamed for apostasy from his
earlier, free-thinking and independent attitude; and
only a little less than the plain language of his
prime do I enjoy the learned diction, elaborate
eloquence, and occasional subtlety of his later style
at its best. But this "best" he seldom attains after
his fortieth year; and the fact that his style, when
he deals with religion, either in its ecclesiastical or
in its mystical aspect, frequently falls into the complexity and artificiality of his very earliest manner has in many minds discredited his motives.
For example, is it to be supposed from the following lines, written in 1818, that he really believed in
angels? And if not, why should he have written
thus?

"Time was when field and watery cove
With modulated echoes rang,
While choirs of fervent Angels sang
Their vespers in the grove."

My purpose is not to discuss his motives, but to
illustrate their effect on his style; and it must be
admitted that in this instance it was harmful. Perhaps it is hardly fair to use this passage as an example, for it is an extreme one; but extremes illustrate tendencies, and the Wordsworth of 1818, when
he wrote the effusion, "Composed upon an Evening
of Extraordinary Splendour and Beauty," had different ideals and different aims from those we find
revealed in the poetry he wrote twenty years earlier,
and his method or technique has changed corre-
spondingly. Earthly, common joy has given place
to visionary raptures; vagueness has replaced precision; loose and imposing words, such as "efful-
gence," "purpureal," and "beaming radiance,"
that he would formerly have avoided, now find
favour in his sight; the double negative, a sure
sign of timidity and monitory age, is not infrequent.

In quantity Wordsworth's poetry equals Tennyson's, exceeds Spenser's, and is about four times
as much as Milton's. In variety of subject-matter,
of tone, and of form, it surpasses that of any other
poet, English or foreign, except Shakespeare and
Victor Hugo, and possibly Goethe. It is to the va-

riety of form in Wordsworth's poetry that I wish
to call attention.

Neither he nor anyone else since Milton has produced a great epic poem. Not the author of *La Hen-
riade,* nor he of *La Légende des Siècles,* nor he of
Childe Harold, nor he of *Idylls of the King,* nor he
of *John Brown's Body* reached that mark. Perhaps "an age too late damped their intended wing."
Allegorical poetry also was quite apart from
Wordsworth's personal character and literary ambition. He admired Spenser without attempting to
imitate him in this form. There was no need for
him to conceal his meaning, and his great and peculiar honour is that he cultivated a direct approach
to truth and an unimpeded transmission of it to his
readers. He produced, without very great success,
poetry of the five following kinds: the Satire, the
Epistle, the Inscription, the Long Descriptive Poem,
the Poetical Drama; and with supreme and characteristic success, poetry of seven other kinds: namely,
the Song, the Story, the Elegy, the Ode, the Sonnet,
the Short Reflective Poem, and the Long Reflective
Poem. I am not altogether satisfied with these categories. There seemed to me a certain impiety, or at
least impropriety, in the act of setting them down.
Many of the poems might be put under more than
one head, and they may of course be understood
and enjoyed without thinking of classification. The

best of them must have been conceived sponta-
neously and composed in a state of rapt attention
to the subject, without much regard, in the early
stages, to distinctions of this sort. Nevertheless,
they can, with few exceptions, be thus arranged;
and it would seem that Wordsworth deliberately set
himself to try all forms of poetical composition
which he felt to be within the scope of his genius.
Few poets have tried so many. With these precaution-
ary observations in mind, let us look for examples:

First, of the Satire. Many readers of Wordsworth do not know that in the obscure period 1793-
1796 he busied himself quite seriously with satires
against the royal family and the government then
in power. Much that he attempted was not completed, and much that he completed was never published. Enough of it is extant, however, to indicate
that he could imitate Juvenal well enough to have
endangered his liberty if the verses had been widely
circulated, though in virulence and audacity they
cannot stand comparison with that master nor with
Voltaire, Dryden, Burns, or Byron. As was fitting
for satire, he used the heroic couplet. Here is a
pleasant allusion to poor George III's insanity:

> "So patient Senates quibble by the hour
> And prove with endless puns a monarch's power
> Or whet his kingly faculties to chase
> Legions of devils through a key-hole's space."

Referring to the Prince of Wales's taste in sports, he writes:

"Do arts like these a royal mind evince?
Are these the studies that beseem a prince?
Wedged in with blacklegs at a boxer's show,
To shout with triumph o'er a knock-down blow?"

Poor stuff, and of value only as illustrating its author's sympathy with the French Revolution.

Second, of the Poetical Epistle. In this he is excelled by Horace, Boileau, Pope, and Burns, and indeed by many others. He wrote nothing to equal the "Journey to Brundisium" or "L'Epître au Roi" or the "Epistle to Dr. Arbuthnot" or the "Letter to James Tennant, of Glenconner," "Auld comrade dear, and brither sinner"; nevertheless his "Epistle to Sir George Beaumont" is full of genuine sentiment and shows the author at his ease.

Third, of the Inscription, or brief monumental poem. This minor form of verse was practiced by Wordsworth with more success. By means of it he connected the names of persons he loved with places dear to them and him. The type interested him, and he contributed to Coleridge's periodical, *The Friend*, a thoughtful and informing essay, "Upon Epitaphs." When that meteoric publication faded out, he had two other essays already written in continuation of the first. Of his Poems on the Naming

of Places, the best is perhaps the lines to Mary
Hutchinson beginning "Our walk was far among
the ancient trees." However, none of his monumental verses are as fine as Coleridge's "Inscription for a Fountain on a Heath," which is the loveliest example of its kind in our language. I can
think of nothing to equal it outside of the Greek
Anthology.

Fourth, of the Long Descriptive Poem. Although
Wordsworth's philosophy in his great period—let
us say from 1797 to 1807—reinforcing his incli-
nations and habits, helped him to understand nature and gather the rich "harvest of a quiet eye,"
he wrote no long poems of which the chief purpose
was description, except "An Evening Walk" and
"Descriptive Sketches"; and it is significant that
these two belong to the earlier period, of intellectual
and emotional immaturity, before he had developed
his religion of humanity and nature. He has no
superior, perhaps no equal, as a descriptive poet,
but his descriptions are scattered throughout his
works and incidental to themes of a subjective character. He composed no long descriptive poem worthy to be placed with Thomson's "Seasons" or Gold-
smith's "Deserted Village" or Byron's "Childe
Harold." He was not only an artist but a reasoner,
and his passionate desire to propagate his ideas
caused him frequently to make descriptive art the

handmaid of philosophy. Hundreds of passages might be cited in which exact and exquisite descriptions of things, persons, and actions have evidently suggested to the poet some enrichment of his theory of knowledge or his theory of conduct. For example, after painting the famous picture of the daffodils "tossing their heads in sprightly dance," he uses it to illustrate his peculiarly high valuation of the power of memory:

> "I gazed—and gazed—but little thought
> What wealth to me the show had brought:
>   For oft when on my couch I lie
> In vacant or in pensive mood,
>   They flash upon that inward eye
> Which is the bliss of solitude;
> And then my heart with pleasure fills
> And dances with the daffodils."

In our whole literature there are few poems that record so much precise and varied observation as "Resolution and Independence." This title might well puzzle anyone reading the piece for the first time, until he came to the last four lines, which give the clue to the preceding one hundred and thirty-six:

> "I could have laughed myself to scorn to find
> In that decrepit man so firm a mind.
> 'God,' said I, 'be my help and stay secure;
> I'll think of the Leech-gatherer on the lonely moor.'"

When Wordsworth said "I am a teacher or nothing," he uttered at least a half-truth.

Fifth, of the Poetical Drama. He wrote one play, *The Borderers*, a tragedy. If we imagine one of the last of the great Elizabethan dramatists—let us say John Ford—looking down from the walls of Heaven upon the course of English tragedy between his time and ours, we may hear him express his astonishment that the grand tree, which flourished so gloriously in his day, has since then produced so little golden fruit. "What can you show?" I hear him ask. "Have those three centuries brought forth a single poetical tragedy worthy to be placed with my *Broken Heart* or John Webster's *Duchess of Malfi?*" If I were so unfortunate as to be the person addressed, I should reply very shrinkingly: "Immortal sir, I am disgracefully ignorant of these matters. There are many plays about which people talk but which I have not read. Yet stay! Our age can claim three poetical tragedies which I beg you to read, for they seem to me not unworthy of that honour. One is *The Cenci*, by Percy Bysshe Shelley; another is *Remorse*, by Samuel Taylor Coleridge; another is *The Borderers*, by William Wordsworth. These plays are as poetical as many written in your generation, and also quite as improbable. They may indeed be burdened with too much instruction, but so, you must admit, are some of Ben Jonson's. They are not unskillfully constructed nor devoid of living characters. And as for poetry, they abound in splendid passages of declamation and reflective musing. There are other dramatic pieces of merit, by poets named Byron, Swinburne, Tennyson, Arnold, and Browning, and a very great one, in my opinion, by Thomas Hardy; but none of these seems well suited for the stage. Like Michael, the archangel, disputing about the body of Moses, you might, by virtue of chronology, claim Milton's *Samson Agonistes;* but I contend that the ancient Greeks have a better claim to that great masterpiece than either your age or mine. If you wish to examine the best full-bodied, five-act, poetical tragedies in the form and style of your time, though written in my time, I suggest *The Cenci, Remorse,* and *The Borderers.* Good-by, immortal sir! Don't ask me any more questions. It is embarrassing."

Up to this point we have seen that Wordsworth tried his hand in five forms of literary art, Satire, Epistle, Inscription, Long Descriptive Poem, and Poetical Drama, in none of them failing, though perhaps in none achieving complete success. He comes off much better in the seven remaining categories.

First, the Song. I distinguish between songs and other short lyrics by the quality of the music. If there is much music in a short lyric poem and one feels when reading it aloud that one ought really to be singing, I call it a song. A perfect example is the joyous outburst entitled "Written in March" and beginning

> "The Cock is crowing,
> The stream is flowing,
> The small birds twitter,
> The lake doth glitter,
> The green field sleeps in the sun."

Then there is the "impromptu," as he termed his gay reply to a half-serious, half-humorous letter from Charles Lamb, in which that inveterate Londoner declined an invitation to Grasmere on the pretense that he preferred the sights and sounds of "the great city," in which he was really "pent" by care for his sister's health. It ends in a jolly tune,

> "Who would go 'parading'
> In London, 'and masquerading,'
> On such a night of June
> With that beautiful soft half-moon,
> And all these innocent blisses?
> On such a night as this is!"

As in the Western Isles of Scotland today, the housewives of Westmorland used to sing softly while they plied the spinning-wheel. There was a belief

that the spindle ran more smoothly when the flocks
that gave the wool were asleep. Wordsworth's
"Song for the Spinning Wheel" weaves this tradition into a drowsy tune. It begins,

> "Swiftly turn the murmuring wheel!
> Night has brought the welcome hour
> When the weary fingers feel
> Help as if from faery power."

Second, the Story. It need scarcely be said that
most of Wordsworth's narrative poems are very
original in subject and spirit. What is not so generally noticed is that the technical forms of most
of them were invented by him. Among the first
pieces he composed after his Continental tour in
1790 was "Guilt and Sorrow," at which he worked
intermittently during the next four years. The plain
diction and simple sentence structure alone would
suffice to show that this long narration was the work
of one in whose mind and heart the Revolutionary
doctrine had found lodgment. It is in essence a
plea for social reform, a protest against war and
social injustice. Readers accustomed to see the
Spenserian stanza, in which this poem was composed, used only in archaic romances, are likely to
be surprised by its entirely modern and unromantic
contents, and perhaps they find the form inappro-
priate to the substance. It is, nevertheless, a touch-

ing and absorbing story, its tone sober, its theoretical meaning implied rather than obtrusively set forth. The entire composition was not published till 1842, though more than a third appeared in *Lyrical Ballads*, in 1798, under the title of "The Female Vagrant." If the whole had been published forty-five or forty-six years earlier, its author's political intention in other poems of his second period would have been less frequently misunderstood.

No poem of Wordsworth's has been so often and completely misunderstood as "Peter Bell," even though it was withheld from publication till 1819, twenty-one years after its original composition, and much altered in the meanwhile with a view to making it acceptable to the public and more conformable to its author's later views:—altered and, I believe, spoiled. As written in 1798, it was probably a more straightforward tale with a more obvious moral than as we have it now. To seek to reconstruct conjecturally its original body and intention is an alluring but hazardous adventure. Beneath much prolix and awkward straining after sportive grace, one can certainly perceive a deep religious meaning and a brave determination to use common incidents and the language of real life in setting it forth. The hypothetical early version was probably altogether serious in tone and its lesson quite obvious and in one respect different from the mix-

ture of Christian teaching with sheer naturalism
which we have in the poem now. Fears and hesi-
tations and a change of heart had supervened, with
bewildering results. What I mean by "naturalism"
may he made clear in a few words. Apart from
those beliefs which they share with the rest of
mankind or large sections of mankind, some prophetic spirits have religious perceptions more peculiar to themselves. Wordsworth's individual
creed, in his most creative period, included a strong
conviction that nature was a kindly mother and
teacher from whom man might learn wisdom. This
is, briefly stated, that doctrine of naturalism, derived in part from Rousseau, but chiefly from personal experience, which is one of the most distinctive features of Wordsworth's greatest poetry. It is
to be found also in many of his contemporaries, and
as Professor Joseph Warren Beach tells us in his
excellent study, *The Concept of Nature in Nineteenth Century English Poetry*, was not only a re-
volt against orthodox Christianity, but a combina-
tion of a rather vague theistic super-naturalism
with scientific positivism, making nature the source
of moral as well as physical life, while endowing
her with divine consciousness, knowledge, and benevolence. However it may be defined, it gave
Wordsworth a profound faith that there was in
nature

"A motion and a spirit that impels
All thinking things, all objects of all thought,
And rolls through all things."

This doctrine, so instinctive and fruitful in some of
our greatest modern poets, yet incapable of proof
and dangerous in certain of its implications, has
been vigorously attacked by the late Irving Babbitt
and Mr. Paul Elmer More and their followers. The
tale of Peter Bell offers them a broad target. He
is represented as a rough, dissolute, unfeeling man,
whose moral reformation is effected through a
Methodist preacher's sermon and more particularly
through the softening influence of nature. There
are many beautiful stanzas in this peculiar and very
unequal poem, for example the twelve of which the
first is as follows:

"He, two-and-thirty years or more,
    Had been a wild and woodland rover;
Had heard the Atlantic surges roar
On farthest Cornwall's rocky shore,
    And trod the cliffs of Dover."

"Ruth" is another religious tale, and dates from
the same period, having been composed in 1799. If
the poet committed himself in "Peter Bell" to the
idea that nature was entirely benevolent, he recants
that opinion here, for though she restored the de-

serted wife to something like sanity and happiness,
she played both fast and loose with the "Youth
from Georgia's Shore," at one time inspiring in
him "pure hopes of high intent" and again offering
him "dangerous food" for his "impetuous blood."

Another group of stories are psychological studies, such as "Anecdote for Fathers," and "We Are
Seven," which illustrate the principle that it is
useless to expect a child, in what Mr. Arthur
Beatty calls "the unreflecting period of life," to
formulate reasons or grasp ideas that are not immediately connected with sense perceptions; "The
Idiot Boy," which uncovers the workings of a de-
fenseless mind; and "The Thorn," which, as Wordsworth meticulously explained in a long, solemn
note, was designed "to exhibit some of the general
laws by which superstition" acts upon men who
have become "credulous and talkative from indo-
lence." It is important that readers should notice
that this tale is all in quotation marks, as being the
talk of such a man. I imagine few poems have been
more generally misunderstood than these four.
People have supposed that "We Are Seven" was a
defense of the doctrine of the immortality of the
soul, and have ridiculed the selection of an idiot
as a subject for poetry, and have overlooked the
fact that the speaker in "The Thorn" is not the
author himself but a superstitious old man, and

have seen nothing at all in "Anecdote for Fathers." But when we learn that they were all written to illustrate certain laws of mental development as set forth by the psychologist David Hartley, the fog clears. As a man of seventy-two, I am inclined to think I know more about children than Wordsworth did at twenty-seven, and I am sure that many "a boy of five years old" and most girls of that age can reflect and generalise to an extent that would have surprised him.

A third and most notable group are long, plain narratives of rural life, which, if we divest the word of its classical associations, we may term pastorals. Outstanding examples are "Michael" and "The Brothers." The characters in this group are real country people, of whom, or of their like, the poet had personal knowledge. He does not employ conventional names and phraseology, as Spenser did, and Milton, and Arnold. The scenes are British, not Greek or Sicilian. The localities are definite. The language of the speakers is neither the dialect of peasants nor the glorious diction of poetic shepherds and deities, but pure and sober modern English. There does not exist a better example of this kind than "Michael," which is thought by many readers to be Wordsworth's most representative poem. In it the modern spirit, the modern standard of manners and character, the modern sense of

moral values, found their first great authentic expression. It is in blank verse, which is well, for it
needs not the jingle of rhyme to enhance its in-
trinsic beauty, and to divide it into stanzas would
have been to break its natural flow. This grand
verse-form, which is peculiarly ours and ours above
all others, was wisely chosen. "The Brothers,"
while not so concentrated and powerful, is also a
great homely pastoral.

A small but distinguished group of narrative
poems, which may be called historical romances,
includes the "Song at the Feast of Brougham
Castle" and "The White Doe of Rylstone." The
beauty no less than the novelty of Scott's "Lay of
the Last Minstrel," and its instant popularity, awoke
in Wordsworth a desire to enter the same field, so
different from those he had till then cultivated, and
his success was an unexpected proof of his versa-
tility. In musical quality both of his romances are
equal to Sir Walter's, and in reflective depth "The
White Doe" at least is superior. Scott's narrative
runs more swiftly, making sharper and more immediate impressions. It appeals no doubt to a larger
audience. But there is in both of Wordsworth's
romances more delicacy of detail and a more inspiring appeal to the higher imagination which
looks beyond the word. The change of metre in
"Brougham Castle," from the swift four-beat

rhymed couplets of the minstrel's song to the slow
stanzas that follow, in which the lines have five feet
and rhyme alternately, is very dramatic and beautiful. The verse-form of "The White Doe" is one
in which composition is deceptively easy and mo-
notony a constant menace. Wordsworth has overcome this difficulty; the story, though feeling its
way through realms of mystery and glamour, has
sufficient variety of tone and action. I would ask a
reader to glance rapidly through its pages, letting
the eye rest only on words of motion or brilliant
colour, words that suggest romantic splendour. He
will reap a rich harvest and realise, even without
reading the poem, that its atmosphere is Elizabethan.

Several other long narratives must be mentioned,
not for excellence, but because they expose Wordsworth's limitations. "Vaudracour and Julia" is
dated 1804 and no doubt was put together then,
but it bears marks of having been conceived and
begun much earlier. It is an ill-constructed tale, the
"events" of which were for the most part foreign to
his experience; and upon his experience depends
that power of conveying a sense of reality which is
his most distinctive gift. It is easy to understand
Arnold's inability to enjoy this prolix and laboured
experiment. I have no doubt that memories of
Wordsworth's own life in France inspired the only
passages in the poem that rise above mediocrity,

namely lines 39-53 and 94-101. By employing
blank verse, of which he was an accomplished
master, he escaped some dangers that beset him in
the narratives still to be mentioned. "The Wag-
goner," composed in 1805, is an unpretentious and
rather jolly imitation of "Tam o' Shanter," in a Lake
Country setting and an appropriate metre, four-
beat lines in pairs, generally iambic, but occasionally trochaic, a form much used by German,
French, and English romancers in the Middle Ages.
The dedication, to Charles Lamb, contains a humorous allusion to that dear friend's pretended in-
difference to lakes and mountains. In 1830, when
he should have known wherein his real power lay,
Wordsworth wrote, *invita Minerva,* three long
stories in verse, stories that have no root in his
personal experience and character or in direct observation. They are derivative and extremely artificial.
Even the versification is unworthy of his genius.
They are "The Armenian Lady's Love," "The
Egyptian Maid," and "The Russian Fugitive,"
this last possessing a certain amount of romantic
or Byronic interest. Can it be that as Wordsworth had imitated Scott admirably and Burns
without absolute disaster, he was now trying to rival
Byron?

Third, the Elegy. Among the numerous pieces
which Wordsworth himself caused to be printed as
elegiac poems, only three possess much interest.

The one in memory of Charles Lamb is a disappointing mixture of pure affection and cold analysis, with here and there a heartfelt, beautiful phrase, but spoiled as a whole by cautious reservations. The lines upon the death of James Hogg, the Ettrick Shepherd, which include references to those other friends who had recently died—Scott, Coleridge, Lamb, Crabbe, and Felicia Hemans—being "an extempore effusion," are free from the fault of over-elaboration which had become habitual with him by 1835. The great poem of this group, as indeed its date, 1805, would lead one to expect, is "Elegiac Stanzas suggested by a Picture of Peele Castle in a Storm." For purposes of biography it is extremely important, because it marks the turning-point of Wordsworth's spiritual life, a change which ultimately affected his poetic art from choice of subjects down to the most minute technical details. For depth of feeling and for spontaneous yet absolutely right expression, it is among the noblest poems in the world. His brother's death in a shipwreck has turned his heart from "the fond illusion" that nature could offer "a steadfast peace that might not be betrayed":

> "So once it would have been,—'tis so no more;
>   I have submitted to a new control:
> A power is gone which nothing can restore;
>   A deep distress hath humanised my soul."

The two poems occasioned by his visit to the grave of Robert Burns, in 1803, seven years after the Scottish poet's death, are even more touching, and the "climbing sorrow" by which great poetry is recognised has always made it impossible for me to read them aloud. England holds out a hand to Scotland in the lines that tell of regret for opportunity missed:

> "Hugh Criffel's hoary top ascends
>   By Skiddaw seen,—
> Neighbours we were, and loving friends
>   We might have been."

Many and strange have been the attempts to trace the so-called "Lucy poems" to their historical and emotional source. It has even been conjectured that, like air-plants or Coleridge's footless birds of paradise, they have no substantial basis. Some of the wisest and most devoted Wordsworthians have made what seem to me the wildest guesses: Coleridge at one time thought "Lucy" stood for the poet's sister Dorothy; my honoured friend and master, Monsieur Legouis, surmised that she was a gypsy; Mr. Hugh I'anson Fausset emerges from a mist of psychological hypotheses with the amorphous conclusion that Lucy was "an imagined being created out of his real feelings for Dorothy and Annette"; Mr. Herbert Read, if I understand his

mystical language, is sure that "the full force of
Wordsworth's adolescent emotions was expended
upon Annette" and therefore she was Lucy; Mr. H.
W. Garrod nimbly and entertainingly leaps from the
Annette to the Dorothy side of the ring, with a
pause now and then before Mary Hutchinson, who
became the poet's wife; and after all he gives the
apple to none of the three. By far the most delicate
and subtle handling of this question known to me is
in Miss Catherine Macdonald Maclean's charming
little book *Dorothy and William Wordsworth*; and
for her, "Lucy" is a transfiguration of the poet's
sister. For my own part I have an unshakable belief that Lucy was a real, an English child, whom
the boy or youth Wordsworth loved and lost by
death; and that the scene of their innocent and
brief romance was that sweet vale where Dovedale
Beck flows into Brother's Water. My reasons for
this conviction are that when the poet was at his
best, as he is in these lovely poems, he drew not
upon his fancy, but upon experience transfigured
by imagination; and that the local and chronological
references can be made, despite one or two incon-
sistencies, to agree with it better than with any
other theory. With somewhat less assurance I think
that to the five generally accepted "Lucy poems" we
may add parts of several others on a fair likeli-
hood of their being connected with the same sub-

ject. The five are "Strange fits of passion have I known," "She dwelt among the untrodden ways," "I travelled among unknown men," "Three years she grew in sun and shower," and "A slumber did my spirit seal." It seems probable that the central and essential stanzas embedded in "The Two April Mornings," "Lucy Gray," and " 'Tis said that some have died for love," are disguised "Lucy poems." I may add that to select these and other similar stanzas has been a "pleasant exercise of hope and joy."

Fourth, the Ode. "Nice customs curtsy to great kings," and when great poets call their poems "odes" we must accept them as such, whether they be of the Pindaric, the Horatian, or some other variety. It is unwise to label a tadpole as an animal destitute of hind legs, for in course of time hind legs appear and lo! we have a frog. An ode may be broadly and inductively defined as a poem neither very long nor very short, of a formal and dignified character, on an important subject of wide interest, and composed with considerable artifice. Let us pass with averted eyes the three wretched triumphal odes composed and published in 1816 to celebrate Britain's victories in the Napoleonic wars. We may be thankful for the victories, yet must despise these productions, which are a disgrace to Wordsworth as a man and as an artist.

Fortunately their style is so involved and pompous, with sentences long and obscured by endless parentheses, that only by hard work can the reader discover how arrogant and callous the meaning really is. The English language has rarely been so tortured or the teaching of Jesus so flouted. The horrible discord of these triumphal blasts seems like a divine admonition not to indulge in militaristic vainglory. The poor quality of *The Star-Spangled Banner,* both words and tune, may be a similar warning to America.

With relief we turn back to a nobler period and nobler phase of Wordsworth's life. Few poems are so complex in structure or have so many changes of mood and tone as the great Ode, "Intimations of Immortality from Recollections of Early Childhood," though it has an air of spontaneity; and few poems are more worthy of close attention. Let us examine its technique. It consists of eleven stanzas, varying in length from nine to thirty-eight lines. The lines vary from four to fourteen syllables. The metre is for the most part iambic, with here and there, as suits the music or the sense, a trochee, a dactyl, or an anapæst. Many feminine endings soften the iambic tread. No two of the eleven stanzas have the same rhyming scheme. There is an exact and delicate correspondence between substance and form. Every fresh turn of thought is indicated by a change in the versification or the vowel sounds, quickening, retarding, emphasising, relaxing, to indicate joy, solemnity, assurance, hesitation, calm. The sudden turn in the music at the beginning of the fifth stanza marks the fact that the poet, after composing the preceding four, paused at that point for three years. There is another abrupt change in both music and thought after the ninth stanza, to introduce a glad uplifting of voice and soul. I have been in a position to realise, more than most people, the difficulty of interpreting this famous poem, because some of the ablest of my pupils, both graduates and undergraduates, in the course of the last twenty years, have written careful and appreciative expositions of it and no two of them have agreed about its meaning. Almost every time I have lectured on it I have myself given a different interpretation. I have arrived, however, at one firm conclusion, namely that its music is our best clue to its meaning. It must be read aloud, and the reading should be a sort of chant. More than any other poem of equal length and value, it would lose if transposed into some other verse-form or translated into prose.

The "Ode to Duty" is less ecstatic, less an expression of moods, than the "Intimations Ode." It is expository. It proceeds by logic rather than by intuition. Hence it is appropriately in a fixed form, its eight stanzas being all alike in structure. After the audacious exploring of emotional and musical possibilities in the "Intimations Ode," Wordsworth might well cry, "Me this unchartered freedom tires."

Fifth, the Sonnet. In a note dictated very late in his life Wordsworth said: "In the cottage at Town-end, one afternoon in 1801 [It was really May 21, 1802, for Dorothy recorded the memorable event on that date in her Journal], my sister read to me the sonnets of Milton. I had long been well acquainted with them, but I was particularly struck on that occasion with the dignified simplicity and majestic harmony that runs through most of them— in character so different from the Italian, and still more so from Shakespeare's fine sonnets. I took fire, if I may be allowed to say so, and produced three sonnets the same afternoon, the first I ever wrote, except an irregular one at school."

He could not have taken fire from a more radiant hearth. Milton, by permitting the sense and the syntax to pass over from the octave to the sestet, and by not making a division at the end of the fourth and the eleventh line, had indeed departed from the Italian practice. I have found, on examining the sonnets of Dante, Petrarch, and Michael Angelo, that in about nine-tenths of them such breaks occur. Milton, the great innovator, freed the sonnet from these quite unnecessary and useless bonds. He also enlarged its application, so that it ranged from private matters to affairs of state. Verily, as Wordsworth later declared, "In his hand the Thing became a trumpet." Inspired by such a master, Wordsworth naturally used the sonnet at first as a political weapon, beginning on that same twenty-first of May, 1802, with his proclamation that a true statesman must be more than a mere warrior: "I grieved for Buonaparté." Although his sonnets for the most part follow the Miltonic model, some conform to the old Italian rules, some are in the Shakespearian form, and others present many minor variations in the order of their rhymes. Taking all these things into account, it appears that he composed about seventy different kinds of sonnet! Readers with very sensitive hearing are no doubt affected, though in all but the most remarkable cases unconsciously, by the slight variations of sound produced by arranging the rhymes in different ways. It is curious that Wordsworth, whose mind was so fertile in subjects for poetry and who was so fond of making technical experiments, should not have begun writing sonnets till he was thirty-two years old, for the form is a favourite with young poets and thousands of tolerable sonnets have been written by persons whom the Muse has not otherwise honoured. Perhaps the necessity of conforming to an exact scheme of lines and feet and rhymes has raised such performers temporarily to an artistic level they could not otherwise have reached. As Boileau says about rhyme, in "L'Art Poétique,"

> "*Lorsqu'à la bien chercher d'abord on s'évertue,*
> *L'esprit à la trouver aisément s'habitue;*
> *Au joug de la raison sans peine elle fléchit,*
> *Et, loin de la gêner, la sert et l'enrichit.*"

Wordsworth, having found the instrument, used it throughout the rest of his life, and I make bold to call him the greatest sonneteer, not only in English, but in any language. If I were making an anthology of the best English sonnets, I should include at least fifteen of Milton's eighteen, twenty of Shakespeare's one hundred and fifty-four, and fifty or sixty of Wordsworth's five hundred and seventeen.

Sixth, the Short Reflective Poem. Of course most sonnets are short reflective poems, and for several reasons this designation is imperfect. Wordsworth himself experienced the difficulty of classifying poems, as is shown by his choosing the title *Lyrical Ballads* for a group few of which bear any resemblance to ballads, and by his unsatisfactory arrangement of his complete works. Yet we may regard as a distinct variety the large number

of short poems, of many shapes, sizes, subjects,
purposes, and tones, which represent his intellectual
and moral character in early life, in his middle
years, and again in old age.

No other English poet has written so many short
poems that are familiar to so many people. Though
they are a miscellaneous group, in a great variety
of verse-forms, they have this in common—that
they all record or reveal some intimate experience
of their author. They are not merely bits of description or narrative, either thrown off at random
or elaborately constructed with a purely objective
intent. Some of them are protests against war, cruel
penal laws, class distinctions, social snobbery. Who
can doubt that if the Wordsworth of 1798 were
alive today he would take his place among the
writers who are representing the labouring man's
point of view, in opposition to our recent masters
and secret dictators, the wielders of money-power?
His voice would not be silent. He would plead,
indirectly perhaps, through description rather than
by argument, for the coal-miner, the farm hand,
the grocery clerk, the garment worker. He would
rejoice in the revolution which is now transforming
this country.

In spite of their great variety, it is possible to
classify the Short Reflective Poems in three groups;
and in so doing I shall not at first mention any that

were composed later than 1800. There were later crops, excellent in form and occasionally noble in sentiment, but not so abundant. The early harvest consisted chiefly of religious poems, social-revolutionary poems, and poems suggested by natural objects and chance incidents and without very obvious ulterior motive. A common characteristic of all these poems is their simplicity. They were purposely composed in the language of common life. Their author aimed to interest, please, and instruct a more general, less learned, less aristocratic body of readers than most other poets had addressed. Another distinction of the group as a whole is the great variety of metres and stanzas and rhyme-schemes employed. The ideas being of many kinds, so are the garments in which they are clothed. The religious poems are those in which he voices his trust in nature as a beneficent goddess. This was an original and personal faith, at variance both with pantheism and with Christian theology. He held it, instinctively and perhaps without much effort to rationalise it, during the most richly productive years of his young manhood. Examples in this kind are "Lines written in Early Spring," "To my Sister," "Expostulation and Reply," "The Tables Turned," and "Tintern Abbey," all of them printed in *Lyrical Ballads* in 1798. Among the social-revolutionary poems may be mentioned "The

Convict," which is a plea for prison reform, and three in which he shows deep understanding of poor and lowly people, "The Last of the Flock," "The Old Cumberland Beggar," and "Alice Fell, or Poverty," this last having been conceived in all probability earlier than 1802, when it was definitely composed. As examples of the poems suggested by natural objects and chance incidents, I need mention only a few of the most familiar to show how varied they are in substance and in form: "The Affliction of Margaret ——," "The Sparrow's Nest," "I wandered lonely as a cloud," "The Reverie of Poor Susan," "The Solitary Reaper." His middle years bore their rich harvest also. Among its fruits are many happy little pieces such as those to the Daisy, the Small Celandine, the Cuckoo, the Butterfly, which all have some reference to human joys and hopes, though without even the slight emphasis on doctrine that is felt in those cited above. To them we must add the deeply reflective "Resolution and Independence," a poem which marks a rearguard action fought by the retreating idealist against the advancing forces of prudence, conformity, and restraint. From a yet later period we may select at least three very fine, short reflective pieces: "Memory," "The Pillar of Trajan," and "Devotional Incitements."

Seventh, the Long Reflective Poem. To a casual

thinker there may seem to be only a quantitative
difference between a short reflective poem and a
long one; but there is more in it than that. To be
sure, some short poems tell us in a very few lines
the result of life-long experience and awaken
"thoughts that wander through eternity"; but there
are arguments that require vast scope for the un-
folding of proofs and examples. The life-story of
a representative human being is the most interesting of all examples, the most cogent of all proofs.
Browning, in some of his reflective and certainly
very long poems, disguises the autobiographical
matter, but it is there, and so, even to superabun-
dance, is the argumentation. The only great English poem closely analogous to Wordsworth's "Prelude" and "Excursion" is Cowper's "Task." Its
quiet, fireside tone, its wealth of just judgments
and calm thoughts, give it imperishable worth and
lift it almost to the level of "The Excursion"; but it
lacks the immense historical value of "The Prelude" and rarely approaches it in sheer poetic
beauty or imaginative sublimity.

As both "The Prelude" and "The Excursion" are
in blank verse and divided into "books," they present a deceptive appearance of similarity in technique. But there is an important formal difference,
in that "The Excursion" consists largely of long
discourses by imaginary characters, the Wanderer,

the Solitary, the Pastor, whereas in "The Prelude" we come into immediate contact with the author's thought and personality, whether he describes or narrates or meditates. The great superiority of the earlier poem is due in a measure to this direct address, which contributes to the sense of freshness and youthful ardor that it imparts. "The Prelude" is unequalled of its kind. "The Excursion," though not so exciting, is by no means a dull or a difficult poem; but its appeal is less general.

I have written all this about the relation between form and substance in Wordsworth's poetry because I am sure from my own experience that the enjoyment of a work of art is greatly enhanced by perceiving and understanding its technique.

WILLIAM WATSON'S POETRY

I ONCE attended the *distribution des prix* at a little
country school in France. To my amusement and
delight every child received a prize, whether for
general excellence or for good deportment or for
"effort" or for gymnastics. All were happy, teachers having avoided unpopularity, parents being satisfied with their offspring, youngsters hugging their
story-books and flowery crowns, the stupidest no
less pleased than the cleverest. Good feeling if not
good scholarship had been promoted in that village.

This may have been well enough for little French
peasants, but it is not the way judicious criticism
awards the prizes for poetry. In the first place,
final decisions are not usually made until after the
long, sometimes the very long, vacation, when the
scholars have dispersed and gone home. By that
time a poet is not esteemed or perhaps even remembered for having "tried hard," nor for the antics
he once performed, playing "such fantastic tricks
before high heaven as make the angels weep," nor
for mere "good deportment" in conforming to approved fashions in versification and imagery, nor
even for "general excellence," a union of admirable

but not extraordinary or unique qualities. No! what alone endures is high or at least eminent excellence, even though narrow; and much more surely does it endure if it be not only high but massive. Time is a jealous judge: Time's tests are strict. He looks with wide-sweeping eyes to estimate the expanse and bounty of a poet's demesne, yet often is content to hearken for some individual tone of a poet's voice; and thus a Sappho, a Catullus, a du Bellay, a Lovelace, a Herbert, a Leopardi receive their no less fragrant wreathes than the blazing and imperishable crown of Homer himself,

> "... quel signor dell' altissimo canto,
> Che sovra gli altri, com' aquila, vola."

Thus far by way of introduction to a brief study of the poetry of William Watson. If it be objected that it is too early to form a just estimate of its place in our literature, I would disclaim any intention of making so presumptuous an attempt, and yet would remark that though he died so recently as August, 1935, he attained considerable distinction nearly fifty years ago, and then, after being much read and discussed for a time, entered a period of semi-oblivion—an interval which gives criticism a certain perspective.

Having enjoyed his company and heard him read

most eloquently some of his own verse when he was
my guest in 1912, in his prime of life and at the
apex of his literary activity and fame, I began recently to read all his poetry and all his prose that
I could find, with the conviction that he had not
received his due of recognition and the hope that
I might enlarge the number of his admirers. During this reading, my opinion of his quality as an
artist and observer of life has sometimes risen very
high and sometimes fallen disappointingly, a fluc-
tuation that has made my task exceedingly difficult.
But the task is important, if I may use so bold a
word; for if William Watson is an excellent poet
it may be worth while to bring his claims to such
notice as I can command. That, taking all his work
into account, I consider him an excellent poet, goes
without saying, or I should not be writing this
essay.

The undertaking is complicated, for he published
no less than thirty volumes and the poems are of
very unequal value as respects both matter and
style, though as a whole they do unmistakably possess style in a rare degree. Moreover, many of them
are remarkable for other than artistic qualities, and
one's estimate of them is likely to be affected by
political and religious prepossessions; not that I
think such considerations out of place in literary
criticism. Judicial balance may be upset also by

attaching too much importance to several personal incidents in Watson's career, which have obtained excessive notoriety, such as his not having been made poet laureate when Tennyson died, and his authorship of that outrageous but diabolically clever portrait, "The Woman with the Serpent's Tongue."

Our effort to discover and appraise the best of his many hundred poems will be aided by classifying them. They are mainly of five general kinds: poems of literary appreciation, epigrams, lyrics, political pieces, and philosophical meditations.

Few poets have written so proudly about the art they professed, or praised so generously and with such discrimination the work of their fellow poets. It was with his noble elegy, *Wordsworth's Grave*, published in 1890, but composed several years earlier, that Watson first became widely and favourably known. He had published, in 1880, a pseudo-mediæval rhymed romance, *The Prince's Quest*, immature in itself, though promising later ripeness for a youth of twenty-two, who had the good sense to study the melodies of Keats and Tennyson. Such expressions as "hoarding the cool and leafy silentness," "gleamy steps," and "melt into the shadow of her eyes" tell us nothing in themselves and much about their ancestry, smacking, as they do, of his models in their unripe years. A volume of *Epigrams of Art, Life, and Nature,* to be considered later, had also preceded *Wordsworth's Grave,* but it was in the latter that Watson revealed for the first time his philosophy of art, and indeed of life, employing an individual style, his own "sincere large accent nobly plain." Nowhere else have Wordsworth's character and aims been so fully and yet briefly summarised; nowhere else can be found a more glowing and yet discriminating tribute to his greatness. I am tempted to quote copiously, but will give only one pregnant stanza:

> "Impassioned? ay, to the heart's ecstatic core!
>   But far removed were clangour, storm, and feud;
> For plenteous health was his, exceeding store
>   Of joy, and an impassioned quietude."

One section of this fine elegy consists of a rapid survey of eighteenth-century poetry, in fourteen stanzas. Memorable is one on Samuel Johnson:

> "In sad stern verse the rugged scholar-sage
>   Bemoaned his toil unvalued, youth uncheered.
> His numbers wore the vesture of the age,
>   But, 'neath it beating, the great heart was heard."

In these closely packed stanzas the vocabulary of English criticism was enriched by more than one memorable phrase, such as "Collins' lonely vesper-chime," and "the frugal note of Gray." Finally,

returning from his excursion through the realms of
gold, the poet comes again to Grasmere's churchyard, which, to use Dorothy Wordsworth's exquisite phrase, "calls home the heart to quietness," and
there he muses thus, in words whose meaning is
more tragic now than when he uttered them:

> "Afar though nation be on nation hurled,
>   And life with toil and ancient pain depressed,
> Here one may scarce believe the whole wide world
>   Is not at peace, and all man's heart at rest."

The death of Tennyson, in October, 1892, drew
from his disciple another great elegy, "Lachrymæ
Musarum." In sumptuous and sonorous verse, rem-
iniscent, it is true, of "Lycidas," yet so expressive
of genuine emotion that it cannot be called imitative, he celebrates Tennyson's glorious and full
achievement, commits him with his peers, the poets
of Athens, Florence, Weimar, Stratford, Rome, and
traces prophetically the progress of his influence
through future ages. If the praise seem excessive,
better so, I say, than the presumptuous, ignorant,
and envious dispraise which of late was fashionable
among a race of petty critics. "Of late," because
the tune has changed again, and if not so rich as
Watson's, is at least more like the song of birds than
the piping of immature frogs. What can be more
certain than the truth of his prediction:

"Captains and conquerors leave a little dust,
    And kings a dubious legend of their reign;
The swords of Cæsars, they are less than rust:
    The poet doth remain.
Dead is Augustus, Maro is alive;
    And thou, the Mantuan of our age and clime,
Like Virgil shalt thy race and tongue survive,
    Bequeathing no less honeyed words to time."

The generous enthusiasm which prompted this comparison will not appear misplaced if we ask ourselves who else, except possibly Victor Hugo, could have been justly called the Virgil of the second half of the nineteenth century.

It is said that Gladstone, recognising the power and appropriateness of this poem, suggested Watson as Tennyson's successor in the laureateship, but that objections were raised by a member of the royal family with whom the poet, while suffering from mental over-strain, had had a personal altercation. Though he was not appointed laureate, a civil pension of two hundred pounds was granted him, and eventually he was knighted.

Another poem of literary appreciation, "In Laleham Churchyard," composed in 1890, is ostensibly elegiac, but almost entirely devoid of any expression of grief. In stanzas which by their metrical arrangement remind us of Wordsworth's infinitely more heartfelt lines, "At the Grave of Burns," also

written in a form which Burns himself immortal-
ised, he passes judgment on the genius of Matthew
Arnold:

> "Its strength, its grace,
>   Its lucid gleam, its sober pride,
>   Its tranquil pace."

Seemingly unaware of Arnold's moral greatness,
his severe toil, his painful wrestling with religious
problems, his combats with theological prejudice,
Watson comes to the chilly and quite inadequate
conclusion that

> "With those Elect he shall survive
> Who seem not to compete or strive,
> Yet with the foremost still arrive,
>   Prevailing still:
> Spirits with whom the stars connive
>   To work their will."

"Shelley's Centenary," a poem in the same metrical form but imbued with a much heartier spirit
and in more glowing language, compares Shelley
with the other two "princes of the realm of rhyme,"
Keats and Byron, and then celebrates him in fifteen eloquent stanzas scarcely less noteworthy for
critical soundness than for lyrical beauty, which
culminate in the following:

"A creature of impetuous breath,
Our torpor deadlier than death
He knew not; whatso'er he saith
        Flashes with life;
He spurreth men, he quickeneth
        To splendid strife."

In lines "To Edward Dowden on receiving from him a copy of 'The Life of Shelley,' " Watson says of Shelley:

"In my young days of fervid poesy
He drew me to him with his strange far light,"

and of Keats, he

"Awhile constrained me to a sweet duresse
And thraldom, lapping me in high content."

But to the piercing tones of Shelley and the languorous melodies of Keats a stronger voice succeeded:

"The first voice, then the second, in their turns
Had sung me captive. This voice sang me free.
Therefore, above all vocal sons of men,
Since him whose sightless eyes saw hell and heaven,
To Wordsworth be my homage, thanks, and love."

In four lines which are often quoted Watson ex-

presses a just literary judgment in words that marvellously fit his meaning:

> "Your Marlowe's page I close, my Shakespeare's ope,
>   How welcome—after gong and cymbal's din—
> The continuity, the long, slow slope
>   And vast curves of the gradual violin."

As an example of deliberate onomatopœia, this
quatrain is likely to find its way into textbooks of
rhetoric. The unconscious kind is of course better,
and though we need not object to an occasional dis-
play of mere craftsmanship, it must be admitted
that in his poems of literary appreciation Watson's
language is too seldom natural and spontaneous.
A cooler head than his and a more restrained hand,
a less passionate heart and a more rigid style would
be necessary for any poet who should attempt to
rival, in our time, the achievement of Boileau or
Pope in versified criticism.

Watson's poem, "The Tomb of Burns," suffers by
comparison with Wordsworth's heartfelt elegy, "At
the Grave of Burns," and comparison is invited by
their being in the same stanza-form. There was
plentiful reason for Wordsworth's dwelling sadly
on Burns's shortcomings, for Dr. James Currie's
depressing Life of his great countryman had only
recently appeared when Wordsworth and his sister,
in 1803, visited the dismal scene of Burns's mortal

decline; but Watson might well have obeyed his
own injunction:

"Not ours to gauge the more or less,
The will's defect, the blood's excess,
The earthly humours that oppress
        The radiant mind.
His greatness, not his littleness
        Concerns mankind."

There are shorter pieces in praise of Coleridge,
Lamb, Landor, Tennyson, Aubrey de Vere, and
Austin Dobson. A volume on Goethe might be
evolved from the four words "Weimar's proud
elaborate calm." On the whole, these poems of
literary appreciation show sound judgment, good
taste, and passionate sympathy; and if their style
is conventional and sometimes imitative, is that not
appropriate in work of this kind? He does not possess Wordsworth's precious and peculiar gift of
reality, of freshness, of immediacy, but we feel the
lack less here than elsewhere. He is most original
in his "Lines to Our New Censor," where he gives
vent to a characteristic *esprit de malice*. They exco-
riate Oscar Wilde, who, "having discovered that
England is unworthy of him, has announced his
resolve to become a naturalised Frenchman." I
quote a specimen stanza:

> "May fortitude beneath this blow
> Fail not the gallant Gallic nation!
> By past experience well we know
> Her genius for recuperation."

Watson poured forth his most scorching sarcasm in *Retrogression and Other Poems*, 1917, upon the formless and often meaningless stuff which even then was usurping the honoured name of poesy:

> "Shun, if thou wouldst by men be heard,
> The comely phrase, the wellborn word,
> And use, as for their ears more meet,
> The loose-lipped lingo of the street."

He for his part, disgusted with such ephemeral fashions, will continue to

> "Seek in deep clefts, and hushed in forests find
> The far-withdrawn Olympians of the mind,
> Nor ever doubt that among wandering men
> These deathless will in triumph come again,
> As sure as the droop'd year's remounting curve,
> And reign anew, when I no more shall serve."

To compose successful epigrams there is needed not only a pungent wit and a bitter sense of the ironic, but also considerable experience in observing human frailty. Watson, with his preference for splendidly coloured and high-sounding diction and his limited knowledge of men and affairs, was not well equipped for the rôle of an English Martial or La Rochefoucauld, especially before he had passed the age of twenty-five; yet in 1884 he published a volume entitled *Epigrams of Art, Life, and Nature,* containing one hundred quatrains, most of them dull, though one is so funny, so unintentionally funny, that I must quote it. Never before or since, I fancy, have ladies been called "billowy-bosom'd fellows." It is entitled "Lines in a Volume of Christina G. Rossetti's Poems," and runs as follows:

"Songstress, in all times ended and begun,
   Thy billowy-bosom'd fellows are not three.
Of those sweet peers, the grass is green o'er one;
   And blue above the other is the sea."

Presumably the last line refers to Sappho, and while it is obvious even to the most unmathematical mind that one and another do not make three, it is not so obvious who the "one" in this case is. With this exception, none of Watson's epigrams can compare, either for amusement or for instruction, with hundreds of couplets by Pope or the author of *Hudibras.*

In his numerous lyrics expressing love, human sympathy, and joy in nature, Watson strikes no new note and reveals no unique aspect of his character, his approach to these subjects being too indirect.

Springtime and autumn, the sea and mountains, foliage and flowers, impress him as they do other sensitive people. He is impelled, as all poets are, to interpret or at least illustrate his own emotions and thoughts in terms of these outward phenomena; this experience he recounts pleasingly, melodiously, and with decorum, but not in language newborn and unmistakably his own. The trouble appears to be that he was not really much interested in the things themselves, and viewed nature almost wholly as a storehouse of comparisons. He reveals no intimacy with what Dorothy Wordsworth called "the goings-on" of the world of outward things. What he sings is not *a* rose, a particular rose, but *the* rose in general; it is spring, a sweet season that returns every year, not one dear, memorable April day that changed the world for him. And so also with his references to persons: we have from his pen few records of actual happenings, few bits of reminiscence, nothing like Wordsworth's "Expostulation and Reply," "The Solitary Reaper," "To a Highland Girl," and "Lines Written in March," or many an ode of Horace and idyl of Theocritus. He can generalise about nature and life in splendid phrases, but lacks the seeing eye and sociable instinct necessary for recording imaginatively facts and incidents of real experience.

In lyrics of a more serious kind, springing from

within, not inspired by natural objects and incidents, but using these only for ornament and illus-
tration, Watson was more successful. "Vita
Nuova," a poem in which he greets life and health
and hope after a dreadful season of "wintry terrors,"
is a very great poem, and contains lines which will
perhaps outlast all his other utterance. Like Earth,
which

> "Claimed with a kiss by Spring the adventurer,
> Wakens, and yields her loveliness to love,"

he now joins the great chorus of "bird and stream
and voiceful mountain,"—he who anon was

> ". . . a string, how jarred
> And all but broken! of that lyre of life
> Whereon himself, the master harp-player,
> Resolving all its mortal dissonance,
> To one immortal and most perfect strain,
> Harps without pause, building with song the world."

Scattered through Watson's volumes, but most
plentiful in the one entitled *Odes and Other Poems*,
published in 1894, are many inward, reflective
lyrics worthy of note for their serious beauty. As
an example I would quote the inspiring conclusion
of the lines "To a Friend uniting Antiquarian
Tastes with Progressive Politics":

> "I count him wise
> Who loves so well Man's noble memories
> He needs must love Man's nobler hopes yet more."

"The Father of the Forest" is an address to an ancient yew-tree which the poet imagines to have witnessed century after century of English history, and which, unstirred by the grim chronicle, replies:

> "Who prates to me of arms and kings,
>   Here in these courts of old repose?
> Thy babble is of transient things,
>   Broils, and the dust of foolish blows.
> Thy sounding annals are at best
> The witness of a world's unrest."

In "Apologia," published in 1895, which we may perhaps regard as a lyric poem, Watson protested against the criticism of those who considered his work imitative, too much concerned with praising other poets, too conventional, too inattentive to the evil passions of humanity, his own included. It begins:

> "Thus much I know: what dues so'er be mine,
> Of fame or of oblivion, Time the just,
> Punctiliously assessing, shall award."

He has "not thought it shame," he protests, "to tread in nobler footprints" nor to find in other singers a theme of song,

> "Holding these also to be very part
> Of Nature's greatness."

With a question which needs to be repeated today, he defends his employment of poetic forms warranted and consecrated by the practice of "the mighty voices of old days":

> "Is the Muse
> Fall'n to a thing of Mode, that must each year
> Supplant her derelict self of yester-year?"

Would that more writers in all time had observed a rule be set for himself:

> "I have not suffered aught in me of frail
> To blur my song; I have not paid the world
> The evil and the insolent courtesy
> Of offering it my baseness for a gift."

There is a noble frankness in this poem, a noble unwillingness to submit, through false modesty, to ignorant and unjust depreciation. He will not deny his kinship with the great; neither will he claim equality with his betters. Above all, he will not yield to the pressure of a degenerate race of immoralists who insist that art should dwell by preference upon whatsoever things are impure, whatsoever things are unlovely, whatsoever things are of ill report.

In his political poems, if anywhere, he made for himself a unique position among poets of his time, and here a stronger passion animates his song. He loved England intensely, praised her splendid qualities, trusted that she would ultimately be true to her high calling as a defender of justice; yet he scourged her for what he deemed her moral failure on several fateful occasions. With the sorrowful bitterness of a disappointed child, he rebuked her for her vacillation in the Sudan, her slowness in checking the cruelty of the Turks in Armenia, her war of conquest in South Africa, her opposition to the independence of Southern Ireland. One is reminded of Wordsworth's predicament when he believed his country wrong in her war with Revolutionary France and suffered in his heart "a conflict of sensations without name." One is reminded too of William Vaughan Moody's brave protest against America's bloody and outrageous suppression of independence in the Philippines, his great "Ode in Time of Hesitation." Many Americans remember the shame with which we viewed our war against Spain in 1898, believing it unnecessary and unjust, even though not knowing then, as we do now, that it was instigated by a guilty group of newspaper owners, armament makers, and excitable politicians. The peculiarity of Watson's position was that with reference to the Armenian massacres he

pleaded for armed intervention, whereas in general
and with reference particularly to the Boer War he
was pacifistic. On every one of these questions of
war and peace, however, he opposed the policy of
the government then in office. His attacks were
splendidly brave and frequently marked with pro-
vocative violence. They made him more enemies
than friends; but that should not affect our estimate
of their poetic value. In fact, the hitherto smoul-
dering fires of his passionate nature found at last
in these bursts of outraged patriotism verbal expression which was the more artistic for being fear-
less and aggressive. At last his defiant and satiric
genius is released; his language becomes less deco-
rous and traditional. Cruelty, of all forms of sin,
is the least easy to pardon. Its hideous roots—fear,
stupidity, superstition—can be traced far back to
the brute ancestry of mankind. When we revert to
war, which inevitably involves cruelty,

> "Our state is as the state of beasts indeed,
> That snatch their meat, one from another's mouth,
> And without pain another's pain behold."

A soul on which celestial light has shone must hate
cruelty. A poet's rage against inhuman atrocity is
therefore honourable and holy. Watson's hot protests against the bestiality of the Turks in 1894,
1895, and 1896, are greatly to the credit of his

heart. In a poet the feelings of the heart have even more authority than the reasoning of the brain. *The Purple East*, 1896, and *The Year of Shame*, 1897, are two little volumes big with curses for the Sultan and reproaches for Britain because she was slow to intervene and stop the slaughter. Disregarding the hard fact that intervention would probably have been opposed by the Czar's government and have caused a general European war, unwarned as yet of the insidious uses of propaganda, and therefore accepting all the horrible stories as true, Watson gives free rein to invective, as for example in lines "To the Sultan":

> "In a world where cruel deeds abound,
> The merely damned are legion: with such souls
> Is not each hollow and cranny of Tophet crammed?
> Thou with the brightest of Hell's aureoles
> Dost shine supreme, incomparably crowned,
> Immortally, beyond all mortals, damned."

Because of his outspoken opposition to the Boer War, he was subjected to much abuse, since, though thousands, indeed millions, of his fellow countrymen shared his indignation, he stood out pre-eminent for the vehemence of his protests. It was, he believed, a war deliberately planned by a few self-seeking individuals and made possible by appeals to false patriotism. Braving public anger, he printed

in half a dozen magazines and newspapers the
twenty-four poems which were collected in 1904
under the title *For England*. They are filled with
grief for his country's crime, forebodings of her
moral downfall, and sympathy with the Boers, in
whom he recognises a kindred race, possessing
those very qualities of which Englishmen themselves are proud. Believing it a war of mere policy,
he sings a dirge for its innocent victims, not alone
Boers, but the British soldiers who died for they
knew not what,

> "Our vainly brave in an ignoble quarrel,
> That fought unhating an unhating foe."

Happily for South Africa, the Empire, and the
World, the subsequent moderation of the victors
and the good sense of the vanquished prevented the
fulfillment of his prophecy to Britain that

> ". . . though she whelm a kindred race,
> A valiant people, stubborn-built as we,
> Yet shall they gnarr hereafter at her heel,
> Secretly unsubdued though beaten down."

After the World War had sickened him with its
horrors and set him to thinking, as it did all persons capable of thought, about the dread possibilities involved in "preparedness" and nationalism,

Watson became a confirmed pacifist. As early as October 23, 1914, in a poem entitled "Tranquil Liberty," printed in *The Westminster Gazette*, he declared that "Peace is no peace when all its dream is war," and prophetically anticipated the establishment of the League of Nations:

> "An areopagus of nations let
>   Men found hereafter, puissant to restrain
>   Flaunted omnipotence, whether on earth or sea
> Or the outraged air, and suchlike peace beget
>   As Tully envisioned; peace itself being vain
>   That is not also tranquil liberty."

His emotions throughout the war are expressed in a volume entitled *The Man who Saw*, published in 1917, the year in which he was knighted. With a few exceptions the poems in this book are typical of the hatred and rage which half the population of the world were at that time feeling or trying to feel. We *wished* to believe evil of our enemies in order to justify our unchristian and inhuman actions. This inevitable and universal habit is one of war's worst curses. Watson was inconsistent; so was nearly everybody. Over against his militaristic effusions, many of which are eloquent enough, may be set a number of more deeply reasoned poems expressing a yearning for peace and exploring the means of obtaining its perpetuity. Indeed, his career is a typical example, acutely painful, of the conflict, now for some time claiming at last the full attention of mankind, between patriotism as hitherto understood and a conviction that all war is wicked, and further, an example of the world-wide conflict between isolation and co-operation as national policies.

Watson published in 1921, in a little volume entitled *Ireland Unfreed*, twenty rather inferior pieces—they are hardly good enough to be called poems—on the vexed question of Ireland's relations with the British Empire. As was natural in a man with an Irish wife, his sympathies were with the majority of the Southern Irish people, but the verses assert little and prove nothing in regard to the rights and wrongs of the controversy. What excited his indignation was the government's unintelligent way of dealing with discontent and rebellion. One looks in vain through these over-heated poems for signs of political insight or any helpful suggestions of a way out of the miserable tangle, in vain for a fair balancing of stolidity on the one hand against unreasonableness on the other, in vain for any appreciation of the fact that Ulster is not Irish in the same sense as the southern provinces and has her own quite different culture. He does, it is true, perceive and note one significant point, which he says "all men that breathe can see," namely that the Puissance which verily reigns in Southern Ireland has its throne "beside Tiber, gazing beyond Time."

Though most of Watson's political poems deal with "old, unhappy, far-off things," there is one at least in which we find "familiar matter of to-day." It was written long ago about the mutual distrust among the great European powers which prevented them from combining to stop the Armenian massacres; but, while our country refuses to join the League of Nations, our consciences must give us uneasy pain when we read of

> "The emulous armies waxing without cease,
> All-puissant, all in vain;
> The pacts and leagues to murder by delays,
> And the dumb throngs that on the deaf thrones gaze;
> The common, loveless lust of territory;
> The lips that only babble of their mart,
> While to the night the shrieking hamlets blaze—
> . . . Of all the evil of which this is part,
> How weary is our heart,
> How weary is our heart these many days."

We contemplate with horror what is now occurring in Spain; and still weary is our heart.

Watson's philosophical poems are perhaps not more characteristic of his genius than the political, but they are, from the nature of their subjects, more expressive of his deepest self and possess a value that is more likely to be permanent, for we have in them, through the medium of a sensitive and free spirit, a report of a vast, uncontrollable movement that was disturbing men's dreams of religious security. His own religious changes are the more significant because they were not mainly the result of reading philosophy or even of receiving the impact of scientific thought, though by the scientific thought of his time he was of course affected, but rather were the reactions of an extremely sympathetic nature to the sufferings of humanity, which drove him to disbelief in God until his heart revolted in the other direction and produced *des raisons que la raison ne connaît pas.* It is not recorded that Job *read* philosophy; he *thought* it. So Watson, in his wrestling with the problem of evil, behaved as the disciple of no gymnastic school, but used his own grips, though it is true enough that no educated person of our time engaged in such a contest can afford to dispense with the aid of science. From his books alone it is evident that Watson grew up believing in the existence and benevolence of Divine Omnipotence, and later, when doubts arose, looked back with a homesick heart to a youth and early manhood of religious faith. But, as he cries in his poem, "The Hope of the World," "not for golden fancies iron truths make room," and he came to believe, most unwillingly, that man's rise from the

clod and the beast had been guided by no foreseeing
mind, but

> " 'T would seem he climbed at last
>   In mere fortuitous hour,
> Child of a thousand chances 'neath the indifferent sky."

Then inveterate Hope protests,

> "When the great bridge is crossed
> Thou shalt behold and know; and find again thy lost."

A less honest and persistent inquirer might have
ended his report at this point, but our poet rejects
the comfort of "a voice so passing sweet":

> "Such are the tales she tells:
>   Who trusts, the happier he:
> But nought of virtue dwells
>   In that felicity.

> "I ask no perfumed gale
> I ask the unpampering breath
>   That fits me to endure
> Chance and victorious Death,
>   Life, and my doom obscure,
> Who know not whence I am sped,
>   Nor to what port I sail."

In a yet greater poem, "The Unknown God," he
turns away in horror from "the mere barbaric God

of Hosts," to seek a Power of which he is conscious, but which he cannot describe. In lines "To Aubrey de Vere," though he protests "Not mine your mystic creed," he nevertheless says,

"My mind, half envying what it cannot share,
Reveres the reverence which it cannot feel."

And in a poem "To One who had written in Derision of the Belief in Immortality" I find what seems to me the most touching thought he ever uttered: he clings to the hope of a future life because he longs to ask of his "dead sire his pardon for each word that wronged his love." It is evident from the trend of these quotations that he was recovering hope if not faith, and we find the consummation in a sonnet "On the Author's Fifty-fifth Birthday," in which he gives thanks for "a perfect spouse," a daughter born to him of late, and

"Deep, deepest thanks that I have now regained
That faith in God which I did lose so long."

In these philosophical poems Watson at last makes appropriate use of the grand style which is the language common to almost all our greatest poets when powerfully moved. He had often used it inappropriately when writing on lighter subjects, and might be criticised for borrowing and wasting the diction of Milton, Wordsworth, Coleridge, Tennyson, or Arnold in their most exalted moods. But here he has a right to the gorgeous epithet and swelling phrase of Milton or Coleridge, the austere line of Wordsworth and Arnold, the golden rhythm of Tennyson. The eternal problem of evil—its apparent incompatibility with the existence of God—and the necessity of solving it at least tentatively if we are to find rest for our souls, has given to poets worthy of treating such a theme an exalted and solemn style. In writing these words, however, I am not unmindful that Goethe, in the dialogues between Faust and Mephistopheles, puts into their mouths the language one might expect from a cynical devil and a disillusioned philosopher.

Since Watson's prose writings are concerned almost entirely with the rules and methods of his craft and illuminate the theoretical background of his own poetic practices, we may not pass them by without a look. Indeed, his literary criticism is so sound, so sane, yet so boldly individual, that it is, I should say, the very medicine most needed today for the fevers and languors that afflict many contemporary poets. The first of his critical essays of which I have any knowledge is a preface to Alfred Austin's *English Lyrics,* published in 1890. It is generously appreciative of these unpretentious and simple pieces, which possess a quality in which

his own poems are deficient, namely, directness of
reference to objects and events in nature and every-
day life. Those who remember the weak surrender
which certain types of literary aspirants made to
the theories of the French decadents about the time
this preface was written will be inclined to pardon
the chauvinism of Watson's remark that "the countrymen of Shakespeare have no need to borrow
either their ethics or their æsthetics from the countrymen of Baudelaire."

In 1893 he published under the title *Excursions
in Criticism* fourteen short articles which had appeared in various periodicals. Owing to their miscellaneous character it is impossible to describe
them as a whole, otherwise than to say that they
praise writing that is substantial and restrained and
condemn in scorching terms what is merely "sound
and fury, signifying nothing." I agree with him in
most of his likes and dislikes and wish he had
turned his fire, during the last ten or fifteen years,
against half a dozen egotistic and pretentious atti-
tudinizers who have hypnotized by their mere self-
confidence many readers more eager for novelty
than for truth or beauty. Some of his pointed say-
ings are well known; for example: "Probably passion plus self-restraint is the moral basis of the
finest style." "Style is the great antiseptic in literature, the most powerful preservative against

decay." "It is the critic's business to feel, just as much as to see." "Mrs. Humphry Ward employs theology to lighten the austerity of fiction." In a delightful imaginary conversation on modern poetry between Samuel Johnson and an Interviewer, he makes the Doctor say: "Yes, sir, Browning could read men. The pity is, men cannot read Browning"—which would be a pity if true. In 1913 Watson prefixed to his volume of poems entitled *The Muse in Exile* the lecture he had given the year before in various parts of the United States, on "The Poet's Place in the Scheme of Life." He had a gentleman's scorn for self-advertisement, an ignoble practice, which, injurious as it then was to the spread of good reading, is far more devastating today; and if there were nothing else of note in his lecture, it would be worth attention for the sake of the following sentence: "We have amongst us the critic with a bee in his bonnet, the critic who finds that it pays him to have a bee in his bonnet, since brilliantly unsound criticism is often more readable than criticism which is unbrilliantly sound."

Watson was an individualist. He fought shy of literary cliques and bohemian haunts. His book called *Pencraft*, published in 1916, is devoted largely to exposing the falseness of certain literary fads and affectations. I wish he had written appreciatively of Walt Whitman's poetry, yet I cannot help enjoying the pungent truth of the following remark: "No great writer ever demanded more insistently to be considered as the natural man addressing the natural man than did Whitman; no great writer ever had a more essentially, I had almost said narrowly, literary audience. His success was largely a capture of the coteries." Blake is a poet I love; I delight in the *Poetical Sketches, Songs of Innocence,* and *Songs of Experience;* yet my reason almost compels me to agree with the critic in his argument that "the wing that rises one moment flags the next; the poem that seems auspiciously born—witness that haunting little piece, 'The Sunflower,'—is strangled in its cradle," because "Blake's Muse was ungirdled and slatternly," that is to say careless of design and detail. "I find Blake wanting," he continues, "while Pope emerges from the ordeal, not indeed a poet of very deep tones or very wide gamut, but an almost miraculous performer upon a rigorously limited instrument, which obeys him with infallible precision and seems delighted to be his slave." Still, I am unconvinced, and feel that Blake's Muse is an angel and Pope's a useful drudge. Then I turn the page and find a sentence so magical, so gloriously poetical, that for its sake I am willing to forgive any critical heresy, and indeed I take it to be a recantation of what preceded: "It is true that the capable and successful, the easy masters of life, are the very last persons to have a private path to the spheres, to have visited the dark side of the moon, or overheard the gossip of the galaxy."

Having brought about this happy reunion of the critic and the poet who together have been the subject of this essay, I withdraw from the scene, hoping that my eulogy may have the effect of adding to the number of William Watson's appreciative readers.

KATHERINE MANSFIELD

"Out of this nettle, danger, we pluck this flower, safety." These words, inscribed on the gravestone of Katherine Mansfield, at Fontainebleau, seem, when one first thinks about the matter, quite unsuitable. She was a woman of extraordinary and amazing genius, a child in the freshness and sharpness of her sensations, a mature thinker who could not be turned back from the pursuit of truth, a literary artist unsurpassed in her special field by anyone of her generation. "Safety," for her, one might suppose, would be a life long enough, with health and freedom enough, to enable her to send forth the children of her imagination, or it might mean that inward peace which is attained by those who find—well, let us say God.

Of danger in her case there was plenty, if there is danger in extreme love of life, in an adventurous spirit, in bereavement and loneliness, in disease and pain, in occasional contact with empty-headed worldlings, on the one hand, and with rootless, fluctuating bohemians on the other, in loss of belief in a God who cares and a soul that survives death. "Danger" in all these forms confronted her, over-

whelmed her, one might think, and certainly killed
her at the age of thirty-four. How, then, can she
be said to have plucked the flower, "safety"?
Keats was

> ". . . content to die,
> Rich in the simple worship of a day,"

and he had good reason to be; the day has become immortality. Katherine Mansfield's day has
dawned, is bright, and will not be brief. Besides all
her unfinished work, there are enough of her completed pieces to establish her fame as one of the
great story-writers of the world. But she cared little
for fame, or kept the thought of it down; so it would
please her better to know, what is truly the case, that
she wrote both more honestly and more delicately
than any other English story-teller of her time, and
opened, or at least widened, a new way of representing life through the medium of prose fiction.
If this achievement be the flower, she plucked it
manibus plenis.

Unity of life, union with life, peace in God's will,
she sought this flower too; but did she find it? Few
of earth's great ones have found it, few of the complex and subtle-minded, who honestly test theory by
experience, comparing one hard fact with another,
and deeply reflecting. Perhaps such peace or faith
is what Milton darkly alluded to in *Comus* as that

"bright golden flower, but not in this soil."
Wordsworth caught glimpses of it, and in the glorious decade when he wrote his best poetry he constructed out of such flashing revelations a new religion, which some people consider very dangerous
and others have found peculiarly helpful in an age
when man's place in the universe has seemed to
shift to a point less near the centre than it was once
believed to hold. Dorothy Wordsworth wore the
flower in her bosom. No doubt thousands of less
celebrated people, who, living for others, forget
themselves, and millions of children and unreflecting childlike adults who take without question what
life offers, enjoy the peace that comes from perfect
adaptation. It is the object of all religion. Katherine Mansfield knew its value. She yearned to possess it. In her very denials of God as the idea of
God had been presented to her, she was recording
her desire for God as her heart suggested Him:
"one wants to praise some one or give thanks to
some one" for the wonder and beauty of the world.
"Whenever I'm praised I always want to fall on my
knees and ask God to make me a better girl. It
just takes me that way." "My philosophy," she
says, "is the defeat of the personal." "There is no
God or Heaven or help of any kind but love," she
declares in one of her letters to her husband, in
November, 1919; and in August, 1921, she writes

to a woman friend: "It seems to me there is a great change come over the world since people like *us* believed in God: God is now gone for all of us. Yet we must believe, and not only that, we must carry our weakness and our sin and our devilishness to somebody. I don't mean in a bad, abasing way. But we must feel that we are *known*, that our hearts are known as God knew us. Therefore love today between 'lovers' has to be not only human but divine." A frail substitute, one feels, and apparently she felt so too, for in a few days she wrote to the same correspondent: "I wish there was a God. I am longing to praise him, thank him."

But, it might be suggested, here were two entirely separate purposes, her desire to succeed in her art, and her desire for union with the All. They were not separate. In her efforts to see things as they are, and reproduce them by her art, she came to perceive with overpowering vividness what she termed "the loveliness of the world and the corruption of the world." A distinct sense of these extremes, their reality, their terrifying oppositeness, is the chief element in all religious experience. And, conversely, those who are possessed by religion are driven to express if they can, in their own medium, that loveliness, and to seek some explanation for that corruption. The more lovely the beauty the more unbearably sad is its incessant and inevitable decay, as Keats well knew when he sang of

"Beauty that must die;
And Joy, whose hand is ever at his lips
Bidding adieu."

Perhaps the cause of the peculiarly intense unhappiness which Katherine Mansfield and many other artists have suffered is that they are too exclusively aware of beauty, which soon falls "into the portion of weeds and outworn faces," and are comparatively inattentive to other elements of life. A botanist, for example, may reasonably be expected to find consolation for the fading of a rose through his interest in those facts of a rose's life which are independent of its colour and perfume. As compared with many other poetical mourners for fallen roses, Katherine Mansfield was sustained by an intense interest, childlike and scientific at the same time, in things as they are, in the laws that make them what they are, in whatsoever determines health and soundness of life. She was therefore no mere æsthete, and assuredly no sentimentalist.

The best of her stories have been published in the volumes entitled *The Garden Party, Bliss,* and *The Dove's Nest,* which contain more than fifty pieces, about two-thirds of them complete short sketches and tales, the others being brilliant fragments of unfinished works. Her Journal, though she did not wish it to appear in its present form but only to serve perhaps as a source for a projected book of reflections, was, nevertheless, published after her death. It was written almost entirely during and after 1916, when she was depressed by the war and the death of her young soldier brother and was herself stricken with consumption. It contains intimate and painful passages which should not have been displayed to the public. There was, however, ample reason for publishing her Letters, which fill two not very large volumes, for they were intended to be read by other eyes than her own in the first place, and are for the most part wholesome and of wide appeal.

This is not the occasion for an account of her life, but the truth, freedom, freshness, charm, and exquisite finish of her stories and the alternating gaiety and quiet depth of her letters will be best appreciated, will indeed be regarded as amazing, by one who knows how she was hampered by hardships of many kinds. She must have had uncommon vitality originally, but by 1915 ill-health had begun to drive her from place to place seeking different climates, physicians, treatments, and residences that promised economy and rest, and following the old siren voices that lure the sick. Travel between England and the South of France was attended by much discomfort and peril; yet after a

dirty, cold, slow, heartbreaking journey, and war-
time troubles about passports and permits, she
would arrive in some attractive place, fall in love
with it, and before the illusion faded, write a story
radiant with sunshine and a handful of letters blithe
as morning flowers. It was, however, a sunshine
lent, not given; her nature was too deep for her to
forget "the corruption of the world"—in Wordsworth's phrase

"woods decaying, never to be decayed"—

and especially the war, which was an instance of
very rapid waste and decay. "The novel just can't
leave the war out," she exclaims indignantly in a
letter of November, 1919. "There *must* have been a
change of heart. It is really fearful to see the 'settling down' of human beings. I feel in the *pro-
foundest* sense that nothing can ever be the same—
that, as artists, we are traitors if we feel otherwise."

The scenes of nearly all her stories are New
Zealand, or London, or the Riviera. The life led by
English travellers in the South of France and in
Paris is too detached and unnatural to provide always the sense of correspondence between environment and human action that Katherine Mansfield
wished to evoke; nor was London congenial to one
who was so often homesick for the country. The

New Zealand stories are the best. And their superiority is due to another cause also; they are memories of her childhood. In her life, so full of geo-
graphical change and spiritual adventure, the real
background, the vivid, insistent, ever-present scene,
was that of her childhood home in the far-away land
of her birth. The liveliest figures in her mind, figures so definite, so bright, so true that it is not
enough to call them creatures of imagination, were
members of her old family circle. They appear in
five stories which may be recommended to anyone
who wishes to make her acquaintance as directly
as possible: "Prelude," "At the Bay," "The Garden Party," "The Voyage," "The Doll's House."
Realism in art has never been more completely
achieved than in these pieces. The people in them
are alive, spontaneous, self-impelled. The reader
forgets that this is fiction. He observes, as if with
his own eyes, what is going on. He fancies that he
too is a child with these delightful children. Everything they do, and why they do it, and how they
feel, and particularly their joy in mere sensation,
he not only understands but shares. It is all quite
natural. They simply could not be otherwise, he
knows. The actual medium of words and sentences
is so clear, so simple, so free, that he is unconscious of it. He does not think about the style, for
there is here perfection of style. An individual

style is often a mark of literary genius. The style is a principal attraction in Stevenson, for example, and in Kipling, and even in Hardy, who appears, however, to be concerned more exclusively than they with character and incident. But Katherine Mansfield is beyond even these great story-tellers in that her medium is invisible. We forget we are reading, and think we are looking on at that family life, in a strange, antipodal, yet somehow very English environment, those childish pleasures, those sudden revealing sorrows and sins, those flashes of noble impulse, the warmth and tenderness of domestic love. The reader will scarcely be tempted to say, *"Et ego in Arcadia,"* for it is actuality, not dreamland, but may well say, "I have been in New Zealand."

These five pictures have been drawn with a freer hand than Katherine Mansfield's other great successes, which are more studied, more definitely outlined, namely, "The Daughters of the Late Colonel" (with an unfinished sketch of the same characters entitled "Father and the Girls"), "The Man without a Temperament," "Miss Brill," "Ma Parker," "The Fly," "The Canary," and the beginning of a novel or long story, "The Dove's Nest." Katherine Mansfield is never false, and therefore one can only feel surprised that in "Bliss" and *"Je ne parle pas français,"* two stories otherwise admirably true, she

should seem to use that all too easy form of literary
allurement, the exhibiting of selfish and base forms
of sexual passion. In several of her letters she pro-
fesses, with manifest sincerity, to dislike fiction
which deals with this depressing and stale material.

In reading our great poets I am always on the
lookout for instances of direct and original observation, such as Milton's "huddling brook" and Wordsworth's hare which, "running races in her mirth,"

"Raises a mist, that, glittering in the sun,
Runs with her all the way, wherever she doth run."

They are not nearly as numerous as one might expect. None of the poets surpasses Katherine Mansfield in the childlike, and therefore poetic freshness and keenness of her perceptions and her frank
report. She is in this respect equal to Dickens or
her great idol, Tchehov. Her eye is quicker, if less
patient, than Hardy's; she sees and tells and passes
merrily on without stopping to elaborate. In "At
the Bay," for example, a flock of sheep comes pat-
tering by, and "Behind them an old sheep-dog,
his soaking paws covered with sand, ran along with
his nose to the ground, but carelessly, as if thinking of something else." His soaking paws covered
with sand—we see him! "Then pushing, nudging,
hurrying, the sheep rounded the bend." "Pushing,"

"hurrying," oh, yes, many a poet has said that; but "nudging," I fancy was never so used before, and it is *the* word. In "The Daughters of the Late Colonel," Kate the housemaid snatches away the plates of those old tabbies, her mistresses, and slaps down a "white, terrified blancmange." "Terrified" strikes the exact chord of mingled pity and humour. When the washerwoman's children are snubbed and driven out of the yard where they have been gazing at the doll's house, the younger girl says softly, "I seen the little lamp," and in its setting this sentence is as pathetic as the justly admired line in Wordsworth's "Michael,"

"And never lifted up a single stone."

These are only four examples out of hundreds that I might have chosen to illustrate the penetrating honesty of Katherine Mansfield's art. Her stories are very simple in outline. "To be simple enough, as one would be simple before God!" she cries in her Journal. And if it be simple to see things as a child sees them, clean-cut, vivid, occupying the whole open, impressionable mind, then she was simple even in the delicate individual strokes with which she filled in the scenes and figures. She rose to a region far above conventional romance, above sentimentality and sophistication, and above conventional realism, with its analytical psychology, and above artistic experimentation, with its self-consciousness, and above the exploitation of temporary interests. Just to see clearly and report truly was her purpose, and withal, to free her blithe heart.

She was, in fact, moving towards the creation of a new literary form, the story without plot. Perhaps it is unfair to say "creation," for she was not the first to make such an attempt. But she stepped forward more bravely than anyone else, and advanced farther. Her best stories have no plots, and some of them no climaxes. It is only now and then that nature orders our lives along lines that resemble the plots of literary fiction. Nature's ways are interesting and surprising and edifying enough as it is. Art cannot do better than to follow her. Some people are beginning to see this, and though when they are tired or sick they amuse themselves with detective stories and stories of complicated intrigue, when they are well they turn to fiction which depicts life as it is, with all its inconclusive issues and undramatic vicissitudes. Dramatic climaxes are rare in life. Character, quality, goodness, badness, colour, feature, movement, are the *differentia* in life, and so they are and must be in mature literary art. Imaginary, romantic landscape-painting, with a snow-clad peak and a gloomy

lake in every picture, is out of date, and there are
abundant signs that stories without "endings" are
preferred by many of the most discriminating readers. At all events it is for such readers that Katherine Mansfield wrote. In almost every instance
the impulse that drove her to begin a story was
purely natural, like a child's interest in some new
face or strange gesture. Then came the desire to
reproduce. If her stories resemble the simple little
tales that Tolstoi wrote for the Russian peasants
after his conversion, the likeness does not include
a predetermined moral in her case. When one has
read that terrible scene, for example, of the man
dropping blots of ink upon the struggling insect, in
"The Fly," something vastly bigger than pity for
the victim begins to swell and cry out in one's heart.
She teaches not by fable but by direct presentation of
experience. She teaches as if unconsciously, like
nature. She teaches by causing us to love persons
and things. She makes us laugh with the joy of
discovering love, the delightfulness of recognition
and sympathy.

Little girls up to the age of eight or nine are
surely the sweetest and most winsome creatures in
the world. Imagine such a little girl, bright and
curious, clear-sighted and honest, and keeping all
her laughing, childish ways, but also enriched with
the experience of a grown woman who has read and

travelled and conversed with interesting people, and suffered deeply; give her also a genius for the use of language; and you have Katherine Mansfield. Genius, and also consummate craft. In a letter of January, 1921, she says: "It's a very queer thing how *craft* comes into writing. I mean down to details. Par example, in 'Miss Brill' I chose not only the length of every sentence, but even the sound of every sentence. I chose the rise and fall of every paragraph to fit her, and to fit her on that day at that very moment. After I'd written it I read it aloud—numbers of times—just as one would *play over* a musical composition, trying to get it nearer and nearer to the expression of Miss Brill, until it fitted her."

A natural, alert, and lively mind is revealed in her letters. They are brilliant, gay, and at the same time touchingly intimate and tender. They show her as a bewitching creature, possessing most potent magic, yet appealing and lovable and making one long to help her. As a letter writer she is to be placed with Coleridge and Lamb. She is even more natural, unrestrained, and intimate than they. Fresh, joyous thoughts were constantly sparkling on the surface of her mind, no matter how sad (but never gloomy) were the depths. Many of her exclamations, little notes of joy from a singing heart, remind us of Dorothy Wordsworth. Like Dorothy too, she perceives beauty and significance in little, unconsidered things. What they see at the actual moment, and what they recall by reminiscence, is alive for each of them; all experience is to them thrilling and memorable and near, as it is to a child. Their honesty is startling; they use sharp-edged words and avoid terms blunted by convention. This is not to say that they do not think by metaphors. For Katherine Mansfield the grasshoppers do not "chirp," they "ring their tiny tambourines." But I like her quite as much for saying, "The craving for a new hat is fearful in the Spring."

She, of course, despises the jargon of cheap present-day fiction, those bastard forms of lazy English and stupid French, such as *tiède, vague, intriguing, troubling,* or for a change, *troublant,* "words which have never really been born and seen the light," as she says. "I have too great an appetite for the real thing to be put off with pretty little kickshaws, and I am offended intellectually that 'ces gens' think they can so take me in. It's the result of Shakespeare, I think. The English language is damned difficult, but it's also damned rich, and so clear and bright that you can search out the darkest places with it." "A little Shakespeare makes one's nose too fine for such a rank smeller as Jack London." Again, in a letter to her husband, she exclaims: "I can't stand anything false. Everything must ring like Elizabethan English, and like those gentlemen I always seem to be mentioning, 'The Poets.' There is a light upon them, especially upon the Elizabethans and our 'special' set—Keats, W. W., Coleridge, Shelley, De Quincey & Co." "I feel I have rather a corner in Coleridge and his circle." And again, she says the one thing she asks of people is that they shall have roots. "The others fade at the going down of the sun. . . . Well, well! The heap of dead ones we have thrown over. But ah, the ones that remain! All the English poets. I see Wordsworth, par example, so *honest* and *living* and *pure*." "I understand Wordsworth and his sister and Coleridge. They're fixed, they're true, they're calm." "There are times when Milton seems the only food to me. He is a most blessed man."

She is penetrating enough to see that Dickens, in spite of his occasional sentimentality and clap-trap, is very real. She finds his novels "adorable," and asks triumphantly, "Doesn't Charley D. make our little men smaller than ever—and such *pencil sharpeners?*" She sends from France for one novel of Dickens after another, declaring, "I am not reading Dickens *idly*." But on another occasion she leaves out even Charley D. and says that only Dostoevsky, Tchehov, and Tolstoi and Hardy are really alive. But this is just her impulsiveness. She is not afraid of inconsistency, and presently writes to her husband, "I have a huge capacity for seeing 'funny' people, you know, and Dickens does fill it at all times quite amazingly." Among the funny people she saw herself and her husband, funny and dear, and she goes on as follows: "As I write to you I am always wanting to fly off down little side paths and to stop suddenly and to lean down and peer at all kinds of odd things. My Grown Up Self sees us like two little children who have been turned out into the garden. There we are hand in hand, while my G. U. S. looks on through the window. And she sees us stop and touch the gummy bark of the trees, or lean over a flower and try to blow it open by breathing very close, or pick up a pebble and give it a rub, and then hold it up to the sun to see if there is any gold in it." To be on the Riviera in war-time, separated from her playmate, was a great trial. "I write to you thus," she declares, "and tell you all because you *must* share it. For the present you are the King in the Counting-House counting out his money, and I am the Queen in the parlour eating bread and honey. . . . Oh, I could weep like a child because there are so many flowers and my lap is so small and all must be carried home."

Enforced separation from the man she loved was not her only grief. I have deliberately kept back till now the note of misery that runs through her

Journal and Letters; for the other note, of thankful gaiety, is rare and precious in literature and more characteristic of Katherine Mansfield. But the composition would be incomplete and its harmonies unheard unless we took into account her laughing triumphs over extreme wretchedness and her dauntless facing of death. It is painful even to think of her bodily afflictions and mental torture, and the Journal is very depressing towards the end. But in the Letters we have a wonderful support from her own high spirits and hopefulness. Near the end, when really she had no chance of recovery, she grasped at a last straw by entering an institute for moral recuperation at Fontainebleau. Here, according to the testimony of her husband, Mr. John Middleton Murry, she found peace at last. But she always liked new places at first, and always wearied of them soon, and very likely the usual reaction would have come this time also. Death came instead. She had been at Fontainebleau a little more than two months, when she had a fatal hæmorrhage, on January 9, 1923.

The flower, safety, was more than the short peace she found there. It was, as I intimated at the beginning, two flowers on one stalk. One of them was artistic achievement. This she plucked and enjoyed. The other flower, union with life, she strenuously strove to reach, and it is difficult for me, and must be difficult for any mortal, to decide whether she succeeded. I believe no one can rise quite high enough to grasp it, to live in complete obedience to nature, to what is best in us, to God. Her phrase, "The defeat of the personal," expresses the essence of what is required. There are no perfect men or women, but now and then comes one who, feeling most joyously "the loveliness of the world" and most poignantly "the corruption of the world," strives more successfully than others to make the loveliness known and drive out the corruption. To do this is to be saved. And Katherine Mansfield did it. What she wrote about her mother is true of her also: "She *lived* every moment of life more fully and completely than any one I've ever known, and her gaiety wasn't any less real for being *high courage.*"

THE END